RELATING
to OTHERS

MAPPING SOCIAL PSYCHOLOGY

Series Editor: Tony Manstead

Current titles:

Forthcoming titles include:

RELATING to OTHERS

Steve Duck

OPEN UNIVERSITY PRESS
MILTON KEYNES

Open University Press
Open University Educational Enterprises Limited
12 Cofferidge Close
Stony Stratford
Milton Keynes MK11 1BY

First Published 1988
Reprinted 1993

British Library Cataloguing in Publication Data

Duck, Steve, 1946–
    Relating to others.—(Mapping of social
    psychology series).
    1. Interpersonal relationships
    I. Title   II. Series
    302

    ISBN 0-335-15339-9
    ISBN 0-335-15344-5 Pbk

Typeset by Rowland Phototypesetting Limited
Bury St Edmunds, Suffolk
Printed in Great Britain by J. W. Arrowsmith Limited, Bristol

This book is for Jamie Duck, who has not had one dedicated to him individually yet

CONTENTS

FOREWORD

There has long been a need for a carefully tailored series of reasonably short and inexpensive books on major topics in social psychology, written primarily for students by authors who enjoy a reputation for the excellence of their research and their ability to communicate clearly and comprehensibly their knowledge of, and enthusiasm for, the discipline. My hope is that the *Mapping Social Psychology* series will meet that need.

The rationale for this series is twofold. First, conventional textbooks are too low-level and uninformative for use with senior undergraduates or graduate students. Books in this series address this problem partly by dealing with topics at book length, rather than chapter length, and partly by the excellence of the scholarship and clarity of the writing. Each volume is written by an acknowledged authority on the topic in question, and offers the reader a concise and up-to-date overview of the principal concepts, theories, methods, and findings relating to that topic. Although the intention has been to produce books that will be used by senior-level undergraduates and graduate students, the fact that the books are written in a straightforward style should make them accessible to students with relatively little previous experience of social psychology. At the same time, the books are sufficiently informative to earn the respect of researchers and instructors.

A second problem with traditional textbooks is that they are too dependent on research conducted in or examples drawn from North American society. This fosters the mistaken impression that social psychology is a uniquely North American discipline and can also be baffling for readers unfamiliar with North American culture. To combat this problem, authors of books in this series have been encouraged to adopt a broader perspective, giving examples or citing research from outside North America wherever this helps to make a point. Our aim has been to produce books for a world market, introducing readers to an international discipline.

The topic of personal relationships is one that has attracted considerable research attention in recent years and this burgeoning research activity shows every sign of being sustained in the foreseeable future. Steve Duck has been highly instrumental in developing theory and research in this fascinating field, partly through his own writings but also through his role as founding Editor of the *Journal of Social and Personal Relationships*. As someone who has been at the heart of the field for several years, he is excellently placed to guide the reader through the latest theories and findings. It is rare for a text to be as up-to-date as this one. It is also unusual for a social psychologist to be so well informed about contemporary research in neighboring disciplines, such as sociology and communication sciences. It is a central theme of this book that the study of personal relationships is necessarily a multidisciplinary enterprise, and Professor Duck does an excellent job of demonstrating how social psychologists interested in personal relationships can benefit from studying what their colleagues in other disciplines are doing. The book is clearly and engagingly written. Those who are new to the study of personal relationships should find it an exciting introduction to the field. Those who are familiar with recent research will find much here that is new and challenging. Finally, those whose idea of what the study of personal relationships entails is based solely on experimental research on interpersonal attraction are in for a pleasant surprise.

Tony Manstead
Series Editor

PREFACE

The field of research into personal relationships has grown enormously in the last ten years and has become an unusual discipline. It is unusual by being truly interdisciplinary; it is unusual by having changed its style of work quite dramatically in the last ten years; it is unusual because of the immense rapidity of its growth; it is unusual by reason of the power it has to speak to issues in real people's lives. It is also *very* interesting: few people can read the research on relationships without learning something that captivates and intrigues.

The question of the interdisciplinary nature of the enterprise is a hobby horse of mine and something I have been working hard to turn into a self-fulfilling prophecy. The issues in the explanation of personal relationships go far beyond the reach of one discipline, even if that discipline is social psychology. The issues are too complex for any one discipline to have all the answers and any biases of a particular discipline's approaches are readily supplemented and corrected by the contributions of other scholarly partners in the research enterprise. In a sense then the discipline is its own motto: the study of relationships works best when scholars relate to one another and are willing to step outside the confines of their own disciplines in reality as well as in prefaces.

There are many kinds of books that can be written "about" a field. At one extreme is a handbook detailing the research that has been done and giving as comprehensive as possible a review of the past and future of the discipline. At the other extreme are the popular books that simplify the research to make it accessible to interested lay people who have no particular training in the discipline but are driven by general concerns or a liking for greater information about a given topic. Somewhere in between there are introductory texts: there are different kinds of these too. One kind fits an area into a broader perspective, such as I tried to do in my *Human Relationships* (Duck 1986) which places the study of relationships in the context of, and in relation to, the rest of social psychology. The present book, on the other hand, is intended to introduce the area of Personal Relationships on its own and in its own right, assuming some broader framework in which the readers will locate it from their own experience and training. I am focusing here on the research strictly in this field and so am aiming at students with some knowledge of social psychology already, or at least some awareness of its principles, even if the reader starts from a background of communication science or family studies or sociology.

This, however, is a book in a series *Mapping Social Psychology*, and is intended primarily for student social psychologists at that. As indicated above, I would not mind if those in communication or sociology or family science or any other discipline also got something out of it. Nor would I mind if researchers rather than students found it useful in its structuring of the literature. Indeed, this would rather reinforce my belief that the topic is a uniter of disciplines and interests as well as a focus of human experience. As a social psychologist myself by training, but one who has switched to communication, I must be honest and state that I fervently believe that allowing the sole dominance of social psychology (when the field was narrowly conceived as dealing only with first impressions or initial attraction) was unwise for the field and helped us to see and understand only some of the major issues. It is because progress in the social sciences not only is built on previous work but also goes far beyond it that we are now seeing the dramatic advances detailed throughout this book. However, this book is for those who might start out thinking otherwise. The book shares some of the traditional biases of social psychology, to be sure. Much of the work discussed here is based on studies of white, middle-class students giving self-reports or reacting in laboratories; most of it is about voluntary relationships (that is, it is not about relationships between prisoners and guards, professors and pupils, couples and in-laws or kin); there is practically nothing here about children's friendships – a topic that I am working on separately (Duck, in preparation). While I cover courtship, there is less here on marriage and on parent–child relationships than there is in *Human Relationships* (Duck 1986). Those omissions do not bother me, given the scope that the book was contracted to have, although it clearly does not cover all the fascinating and profound relationships that could be studied. (The *Handbook of Personal Relationships* is some 700 pages long and does not exhaust the topics either).

Given these admitted limitations, the book offers a perspective on the science of personal relationships that is broadly based on the historical development of the discipline from its roots in social psychology toward the broader canopy that it now sports. It traces the early work on attraction to strangers through the work on physical attractiveness and then moves on, as the field has done, to consideration of the broader work that now characterizes the discipline, in terms of continuing real-life relationships that develop or deteriorate, taking account of social context and communication patterns as well as the internal emotional experience of the individuals in a particular dyad. My hope is that this will show not only the contribution made by social psychology to the study of relationships but also the ways in which social psychology can learn from and build on the work of other scholars by opening its mind to the value of the work that they do. Since the finishing touches to the book were made during the first Iowa Conference on Personal Relationships, where several leading workers in the field of personal relationships and in social support interacted for the first time to their mutual benefit, I know that the initial approach to the idea of openness to interdisciplinary work is scepticism and shouts of "naivety"; but I also learned, as I had hoped, that the outcome is nevertheless conversion to the idea.

This field is so exciting because it is now progressing and proving its worth as a scholarly pursuit. It is, I believe, poised for major recognition and growth within and across several disciplines. In my opinion it will also be the major field in social psychology, akin to attribution theory, by the mid-1990s. My colors thus incautiously nailed to the mast, I now invite you to see for yourself whether you will agree with me.

ACKNOWLEDGEMENTS

I am grateful to many people who have helped me with this book. Foremost is my secretary, Chris Brenneman, who worked like a Trojan in spite of my famous handwriting, and never let me down once on impossible deadlines or unreasonable tasks while she also completed all the possible and reasonable ones ahead of time. I really could not have managed to do the book without her unstinting help and assistance (and quite often guidance and correction as well).

Roz Burnett did an excellent job of reading the first draft and producing well-judged and extremely helpful comments that made the book a better product than it would otherwise have been. Dan Perlman, Keith Davis, Paul Wright, and Bob Milardo read the final manuscript (as I thought) and made such careful, attentive, and well-judged comments, coupled with such good guidance for revisions, that I could not ignore them and just had to write the "final version" again. Mollie Condra and Tony Manstead also read and commented on the drafts and I benefited very greatly from their thoughtful and detailed advice. Joanna Lawson helped me with both final versions of the manuscript and gave support and encouragement when the going got rough. I am grateful to all of these people for their help.

I also hereby acknowledge with thanks the permission of Academic Press Inc to reproduce Figure 1 from T. L. Huston *et al.*'s chapter in S. W. Duck and R. Gilmour (eds) *Personal Relationships 2: Developing Personal Relationships*, London and New York: Academic Press, p. 77; Figure 2 from S. W. Duck (ed.) (1982) *Personal Relationships 4: Dissolving Personal Relationships*, London and New York: Academic Press, p. 16, and Figure 3 from S. W.

Duck (ed.) (1984) *Personal Relationships 5: Repairing Personal Relationships*, London and New York: Academic Press, p. 169. Finally, I acknowledge the gracious permission of Guilford Press for me to borrow extensively from my article with Harriet Sants in Chapter 8. Some of the ideas there were first published in Duck and Sants (1983) "On the origin of the specious: Are personal relationships really interpersonal states?" *Journal of Social and Clinical Psychology*, 1, 27–41.

1 / THE ROLE OF RELATIONSHIPS IN LIFE

That personal relationships and friendships are important to us is obvious. We need merely to reflect for a moment on the sources of our greatest pleasure and pain to appreciate that nothing else arouses the extremes of emotion that are experienced in the course of personal relationships with other human beings. If formal evidence were needed, however, it is to be found in a report by Klinger (1977) which surveyed "inner experience and incentives in people's lives." The clear leader was people's relationships with one another: almost everyone indicates that it is important to feel loved and wanted. For the majority of people, the answer to the question, "What is it that makes your life meaningful?" is one that refers to close relationships with friends, kin, their children, or life partner. Recent work by Argyle (1987) confirms this and notes that, by contrast, money, career, and religion are relatively less important for people than are their personal relationships. Equally, and conversely, there is now considerable evidence that the presence of a close confidant helps to stave off not only depression (Brown and Harris 1978) but also other clinical problems (O'Connor and Brown 1984) and certain physical ailments (Reis 1984).

Poets, novelists, playwrights, philosophers – and many other besides – have studied relationships in an effort to discover why they matter, how they work, and how to improve their quality. Even ancient Greeks like Aristotle and Roman orator-philosophers like Cicero had something to say about relationships with other people, particularly friendships. Despite all the years devoted by such thinkers to the problems of explaining and improving friendships, marriages, and social relations in general – even international relations – we are only just beginning to find out the answers to broad questions in our own personal lives. Common sense is not a good assistant here: it offers merely uncertainties and conflicting advice ("opposites attract" yet "birds of a feather flock together," for instance). Such maxims should prompt scientists to ask a host of more complex questions. Not only should we begin to ask which factor matters most, similarity or oppositeness, but also what kinds of similarity or oppositeness, and in what way do they matter? Do they cause initial attraction or do they promote good relationships in the long term? What kinds of relationships do they affect? What ages of subjects are most relevant? Do they work all the time or only in some circumstances? And so on. It is perhaps because common sense is not much help that questions about the proper way to conduct everyday relationships seem to constitute the bulk of issues raised in problem pages, self-help courses, and intimate confessionals, as well as occupying the minds of all of us at some time or another.

The development of the field of research in personal relationships

To make a contribution to knowledge that will provide practical advice on the successful conduct of relationships, social science as a whole has turned its concerted attention to personal relationships only recently – since about the start of the 1980s – although work on specific kinds of relationships, like marriage, has a longer history in family studies. Indeed, in the grand historical context, the scientific scrutiny of social and personal relationships has been so recent a development that it is still only a viable fetus: not yet even in its infancy. Nevertheless, many common-sense assumptions have been put to the test in empirical research, the truths thereby being separated from the half-truths and the cosy errors, as I shall try to show in the rest of this book.

As will be apparent from the suggestions for further reading at the end of this chapter and subsequent chapters, there is now no shortage of social psychological and other social scientific works devoted to personal relationships. Whereas work used to focus mainly on why we are attracted to strangers (e.g. Berscheid and Walster 1978; Byrne 1971; Duck 1977b), it now extends to investigation of methods of exploring real-life, long-term relationships (Duck and Gilmour 1981a; Duck and Sants 1983; Harvey *et al.* 1988; Ickes and Tooke

1988; Kenny 1988; Patterson 1988); it looks at the features that identify "best friendship" and distinguish it from, say, casual acquaintance or marriage or "ordinary" friendship (K. E. Davis and Todd 1985; Perlman and Fehr 1987; Hays 1988); it addresses the question of how relationships develop and change (Baxter and Wilmot 1986; Delia 1980; Duck and Gilmour 1981b; Duck and Miell 1986; Huston *et al.* 1981; Perlman and Fehr 1987; Perlman and Duck 1987); and it deals with the problems of relationship dissolution and decline (Duck 1982b; Hagestad and Smyer, 1982; G. J. McCall 1982). While such research typically takes a relatively traditional social psychological approach (often being carried out as survey research or laboratory study, for instance), there is a move toward field observation (for example Sants 1984 studied children's relationships in the school playground) and the relating of personal characteristics to actual experiences in friendship and social participation (for example Reis *et al.* 1980 studied the social participation of attractive persons; and McAdams 1988 examined the role of a person's needs and personality/motivational structure in friendship).

In part this progress is due simply to the immense growth and focusing of relevant research in recent years and to the greater methodological sophistication that has come through cross-disciplinary interaction. Researchers from several disciplines have brought their expertise to bear on the issue of relationships, the most prominent being sociologists, social psychologists, clinicians, developmental psychologists, family scientists, and communication scientists. Yet it is only since 1984 that workers in these disciplines have been able to communicate their research to one another via the multidisciplinary channel of the *Journal of Social and Personal Relationships*. Furthermore, there are now several series of books and various conferences focused on personal relationships. Developments such as these have stimulated growth in research, enhanced the intensity with which particular issues are studied, and encouraged the development of new styles of research. They have done this by bringing researchers together as an identifiable community working on agreed problems rather than as isolated individuals researching and publishing in an engulfing environment with research agendas driven by colleagues who had other primary interests.

One reason for the recent intense excitement in the field of personal relationship research is the very fact that progress is becoming rapid as we move from the style of work that remains in the laboratory environment (see Chapters 1 and 2 here, as well as

Burnett *et al.* 1987; Duck 1985; Duck 1986; Duck and Perlman 1985; and Rychlak 1984, for fuller discussion of these points and the reasons for recent changes in the style of research).

Nevertheless, it is my belief that from time to time specific topics in social psychology just happen to become the target of dramatic surges of interest, and that this happens almost unaccountably as the *Zeitgeist*, or the spirit of the time, dictates – rather like popular music and the fashions of different generations. As I have argued elsewhere (Duck 1980b), that *Zeitgeist* is shaped by people, rather than being some disembodied ghost in the research machine. It is the decisions and actions of theorists and researchers – and their students – that promote some fields of activity while causing others to decline. The field of personal relationships research is lucky enough to have not only interesting problems to address but also a range of improving solutions to them, in addition to a young and vigorous group of researchers who are likely to make the field attractive to those working in other fields and thereby establish themselves as part of the *Zeitgeist*. I am therefore confident that the present growth of interest in personal relationships indicates that it is destined to become a key area of research in the 1990s.

A book such as this – especially since it is intended to be concise – therefore has quite a task before it in giving a fair representation of the historically important work while keeping the present styles in mind, since they are such different extensions of what came before. While you will read here about the laboratory research that characterizes much of social psychology, you will also be introduced to the more varied techniques that derive from other disciplines and take us further into the real world where people conduct their daily lives. These other disciplines have important contributions to make but, of course, they do not tackle precisely the same questions or use precisely the same techniques as social psychologists do. Sociologists, family scientists, and communication scientists do not think in the same terms as social psychologists and therefore approach problems and their solutions differently. But just as an athletics team will not win the Olympics if it consists only of high-jumpers and nobody who can sprint or throw a javelin, so cooperation between disciplines is needed to increase our knowledge on wider fronts.

This book will therefore cover more research than that narrowly encompassed in traditional social psychology and associated traditional social psychology textbooks – not only because I believe that social psychologists do not know all there is to know about relating to other people, but also because social psychological research can benefit from the contributions of other disciplines as much as vice versa. On the other hand, I emphasize the social psychological approach, tinged strongly with communication theory. That is to say, I am writing about the ways in which people think about social events, the nature of interpersonal interaction face-to-face, the individual and social forces that affect communication in social interaction, and the thoughts, feelings, and actions that make up the process of relating to others.

Such an approach can be applied in a general way to relating to others, since many researchers believe that there are general principles in social and personal relationships, even if there are also particular defining characteristics for each sort of relationship. Thus, while we shall see that casual and best friendship are somehow the same, they are also different in some respects. For example, both involve interaction, mutual liking, and probably trust, yet best friendship also manifests levels of intimacy and concern for one another that are less evident in casual friendship. Equally, while dating partners do many things, and are many things, to each other that married couples, close friends, and acquaintances do and are, there are qualities that nevertheless differentiate these four kinds of relationships. My argument throughout this book will essentially be that the differences and the similarities are both to be found in the extent to which, and the ways in which, the lives of the two partners are intertwined.

Life's rich pageant of little things

In order to understand more clearly just why it is that relationships are voted the most important aspect of our lives in a general sense, we need a clear picture of the role of relationships in our everyday lives in a particular sense. Even if we all believe that personal relationships are a "Good Thing," how do they work in reality? How does friendship map on to everyday life? What do friends actually do for us? Is our time with others spent looking meaningfully into a mystical sunset, or is it spent drinking coffee together, talking about our shopping needs, arranging to play tennis, and complaining about colleagues at work? Also, in coming to understand the significance of relationships, we need to understand more clearly the role of everyday life events in our relationships. However grand our motives are supposed to be by philosophers and religious writers, at bottom most of our daily life is mundane ("the long littleness of life," as Frances Crofts Cornford called it) – and it is that process of social living that social psychology is all about, not simply what people do in special, interesting, and involving circumstances in laboratories. We therefore need to explore the underpinnings that social relationships provide for the rest of social behavior and hence for social psychology (see Duck 1980b and 1986 for the full argument of this point).

It is very clear, but often under-appreciated, that daily events are typically centered on and intertwined with our relationships in remarkable ways. It is so obvious as to be unremarkable that many of our most significant meetings are with friends or family; many of our major concerns are about relationships or about the people with whom we share them; many of the most fearful and life-shaking crises concern the separation of ourselves from our friends or relatives (for example divorce and separation from children, bereavement, estrangement, leaving home, the ending of love affairs). More subtle, more important, and less clearly understood than these dramatic and cataclysmic instances, however, are the other more frequent and typical cases, where apparently minor daily events impinge upon our relationships and vice versa. For example, daily life at work or at play brings us into contact with many people we like and dislike only moderately, but they affect our enjoyment of and attitudes to life; we gossip about other people (Emler and Fisher 1982), we form our relationships, we share our experiences in ways that seem to enhance our psychological health and our sense of well-being (Reis 1984) – and we do it through the medium of relationships. But not all of this results in lofty enterprises. The boring human chores that make up much of our everyday existence have also to be incorporated into our relationships. Thus we go shopping with a companion, get others' advice about what to buy or to wear, or ask a friend's help in shifting a piano. We eat meals with friends and relatives; we watch television with companions; we make both big and small decisions with the advice of confidants; we wash the dishes and cook with or for intimates; we take our leisure, play our sports, watch our football games, and go to the movies with friends. We even go to classes with people whom we know, arrange our timetables around shared human needs like food, and organize our lives around joint ventures and projects like leisure and sports, or shared desires, like sex. We structure our relationships in various ways to accommodate our daily human requirements for staying alive, keeping our bodies functional and healthy and stimulating or recreating ourselves.

While all this may seem trivial to us (and certainly used to seem trivial to researchers), a moment's reflection will show us that relationships are affected by these things in more than minor ways. For one thing, many of these trivial tasks and ventures require not only joint planning and agreement about priorities, but also co-ordination of personal schedules that may otherwise be more or less unrelated (Clarke *et al.* 1986). The less involved two people are, the more it is difficult to manage such coordination of their unrelated daily lives and yet as we get to know someone better not only do we want to spend more time with them, but also we usually become more accessible to them as part of the role. We are supposed to "be there" whenever a friend needs us and inaccessibility has to be explicated and excused. Non-availability is unfriendly and under-mines the sense of relationship. Even so, the necessary discussion or planning may be beyond the resources of the partners or may get them into heated discussion that could affect the future of the relationship or its development. For instance, couples frequently get into conflict about when they should be ready to go out or the amount of time that can be devoted to work and to leisure; others argue about the coordination of desires for sexual behavior or where to go out when, or who does what around the house, or whose turn it is to go out shopping or what TV program to watch. These conflicts can be major or trivial (or can start by being trivial and turn into something bigger) but they are most definitely not irrelevant to satisfaction in the relationship. They may even affect the whole nature and course of the relationship, despite the fact that they seem superficially to be utterly immaterial to it.

As a related point, consider that the creation, organization, or development of a relationship may place the two persons in conflict with other people or parts of their life – as when the birth of a child brings the new parents into conflict as they attempt to adjust (Lips and Morrison 1986), or when one falls in love with someone at work in contravention of stated university policy about student–instructor relationships, or when one likes a person of whom one's parents disapprove, or when a friendship or love affair is so strong and important that it makes one reluctant to take an offer of promotion or a new job.

Researchers need to consider not only the events that clearly take place within a relationship (for example what makes one person feel liking for another, or the intimacy level in a relationship), but also the events and circumstances that impinge on the relationship from outside, such as the pressures of daily living, the contexts and circumstances that affect the relationship, the effects of belonging to a particular culture, with its own rules and definitions of relationships, the influence of being in a network of other people within which the relationship occurs, and so on. In short I think it is necessary to explore not only the interior affective elements in a relationship but also the exterior context. I regard the simple and ordinary business of living as an important element of this context.

What are the relevant features of everyday life?

There is very little in everyday life that could not be relevant in some way to a person's experience and enjoyment of personal relationships, given the above remarks. One way of looking at it is to recognize that the sharing of close relationships involves the sharing of our lives, not just our feelings, and that our lives are made up of all that humans think, feel, experience, and do.

Relationships do not just happen in a vacuum: they occur in a context provided not only by various human needs that relationships satisfy and that direct relational behaviors, but also by exterior elements that impinge on people's choices and freedom to exercise them, such as the prevailing cultural rules (which, of course, can become internalized). To focus this a little, however, I shall identify three main areas of concerns that seem to be especially relevant: (1) the interior, cognitive/emotional elements of individuals; (2) the exterior factors and influences like time and culture; (3) other factors such as individual skills at relating, the role of chance, opportunity, and coincidence in relating.

Interior needs and concerns of human beings

We naturally assume that the most important factor in our relationships is whether we like, dislike, or feel neutral about the people whom we meet. It probably also occurs to us as natural that feelings would be the most important factor in the growth and development of relationships. However, this view is insufficient. For one thing, our

feelings are affected by various human needs and social circumstances (cf. P. H. Wright 1984; 1985 for a list of the needs identified
by his long and impressive research program, discussed here in
Chapter 3). For another, our personality style may influence the
kinds of relationships that we seek out and the reactions that we have
to intimacy (cf. McAdams 1988, who shows that some groups of
people have strong needs for warm, close interaction with others
while some people do not, and that the two groups' friendships
reflect those underlying needs; and also Hazan and Shaver 1987,
who indicate that people's recollections of their childhood attachments to their parents can be reflected in the sorts of relationship that
they establish with other adults when they are themselves mature). In
short, our feelings towards others are not "absolute" influences on
our relationships but depend on, and are influenced by, our own
personality, personal needs, and past relational experiences. Furthermore, our feelings alone do not create relationships for other
reasons. For instance, we may feel that we like someone but be
uncertain about their corresponding feelings for us, so we decide not
to act on our own feelings as, for example, Duck and Miell (1986)
found (see next section). Or we may love someone very strongly but
feel inhibited in showing it because of what our friends, colleagues or
even the law might think about it (G. J. McCall 1970). Also we may
feel that we want to develop a relationship but go about it in an
unskilled way (Argyle 1983) or be too shy to make the right moves in
the right way. These are some – only some – of the reasons why
feelings alone are not enough.

Uncertainty

A clear but under-researched fact about human social life is that we
are very often uncertain about others' feelings for us. (By contrast,
researchers have devoted a great deal of time to unraveling our
attributions about why other people do things rather than how they
feel towards us). In a study I did with Dorothy Miell (Duck and Miell
1986) it was found that individuals starting relationships were very
uncertain about their partner's feelings for them and tended to
underestimate the stability of the relationship and their own role in
it. It is as if subjects acted on the assumption that it is the other person
who controls, and is responsible for the existence of, the relationship,
and that if the other person changed his or her mind, the relationship

would disintegrate, whatever they thought of it themselves. Subjects saw others as their friends rather than claiming to be sure that they themselves were someone else's friend.

This general and very pervasive uncertainty leads to certain predictable behavior and thought patterns in people and results in an "effort after meaning" (Berger and Bradac 1982). A large part of the development of relationships is a dogged attempt to gain information about the other person and his or her likely relationship to oneself (Bradac 1983). We seek information that helps us to interpret the other person, to form an impression of him or her, to reduce our uncertainties about him or her, and reassure us that he or she might make a good partner for us (these issues will be discussed more thoroughly in Chapters 2 and 3).

Projects

One consequence of this effort after meaning is a need for structure in life and a way of achieving this is by having projects to accomplish. Little (1984) has pointed out that we all have both mini-projects and maxi-projects that help to structure our lives. We may, for example, be concerned about petty, pressing matters like a need to tidy the house before guests arrive, or to get good grades on a class assignment, or we may be focusing on a more impressive life project like "Be a better friend to Joanna" or "Teach Jamie to read" or "Learn to express emotions" or "Behave more assertively." Such projects probably occupy a lot of cognitive capacity and intrude into our social concerns and social behavior in ways that direct and influence what we do or think. For instance, the urgency of a small project may prevent us from taking long enough to deal with a friend's need for advice or help on a given occasion, or our pressing thoughts and concerns may keep creeping into our conversation with a friend, or may affect the ways in which we happen to structure our time during the day, or could influence the ways in which we choose to act in a given meeting with a new acquaintance (for instance, by being very friendly and available if we have just moved to a new town and have begun a project to "make more friends"). As such, these projects obviously have impact on our social and personal relationships both directly and indirectly. Although the possibility that they do so is rarely studied, such concerns are likely to be important motivations and influences on much of our social behavior (Little 1984). They make up a large part of being human, and as such, go with us wherever we go and enter into all our social interactions.

Inclusion

A major project that we need to fulfill and for which we seek others' company is need for inclusion. Needs of human beings for inclusion amount essentially to a need to be part of a social structure, a need to feel we belong, a need to experience life as a part of a community or network of others, however small that community may be (Weiss 1975). Each of us has desires for membership of pairings, groups, and networks, and a large part of our concern in friendship development is for establishment of such inclusion. It ratifies us as people – that is to say, it shows us that we are acceptable to other people in the things that we do, the ways that we think, the emotions that we feel, the concerns that we have, and the solutions that we propose to problems in our own and others' lives. It gives us a social value, the chance to evaluate ourselves by comparing ourselves and our reactions with other people and their reactions. It also gives us a chance to see ourselves as important to at least one other person in the world. To be included is to be accepted and to be accepted is (both implicitly and explicitly) to be approved. Exclusion is a social means of registering disapproval. It says, "We don't want you; you're no good; you're not acceptable as a human being." That is why it is painful to feel left out and why loneliness hurts so much: it conveys the message to the rejected or lonely person that he or she is not to be included, not to be accepted, not worth very much to anyone else.

There are large research programs that have investigated the differences between individuals in the need for inclusion or need for affiliation (e.g. Mehrabian and Ksionzky 1974; Schachter 1959) and it is clear that there are differences between people (for example Goldstein and Rosenfeld 1969 found that neurotics, to a much greater extent than other people, find it difficult to tolerate dissimilarity in other people and find it stressful – at least to begin with – to affiliate with others who are not from the same background as themselves and who do not share the same attitudes: they find dissimilarity inordinately threatening in early encounters). It is also clear that circumstances can determine the need for friendship, with people generally preferring company while they are under stress (Schachter 1959). Such research programs and their evaluation could well take up a whole chapter or take us into the issue of social support and its psychological nature (cf. Cobb 1976; Duck 1983; Gottlieb 1988; Hobfoll and Stokes 1988). My purpose here is introductory rather than exhaustive, so I emphasize that my point is only that the need for inclusion is generally important to all of us, however that basic importance may be affected by personal idiosyncrasies, ecological stress, or circumstantial variation. Humans like to relate to other people.

Similarity

Another consequence of the uncertainties of social life is that we prefer, to a greater or lesser extent depending on personality style, similarity to dissimilarity. We all have a preference for the familiar over the unfamiliar (cf. Kerckhoff 1974). When it comes to choosing mates and friends, we pick from a "field of eligibles" that is already much filtered and reduced by this human reaction to a human need. Thus Kerckhoff (1974) notes that married partners typically come from the same race, the same social class, the same religion, the same socioeconomic background, the same intelligence level, and the same educational context. It is even likely that persons will marry others who live within a very small distance from themselves (cf. Fischer 1982; Blumstein and Schwartz 1983). Preference for the similar and the familiar over the rest manifests itself in the tendency to mix and associate with people from the same background as ourselves: we prefer other people with attitudes similar to our own, and we feel comfortable with people who share some of our characteristics (Kerckhoff 1974). It is axiomatic in research on friendship and relationships that we seek out others who have something in common with us, but it is not always recognized that this is probably based on our need for inclusion and our concerns that we be members of a community of equals (Weiss 1975).

Memory for social experience

Memory for social experience serves our human needs too. The ways in which we remember social events, social interactions, friendships, and relationships are important because memory not only records experience but also organizes it in ways that are personally relevant and meaningful, especially in our memories of relationship events (Burnett et al. 1987; Harvey et al. 1982; 1986). Memory is not always purely "photographic" but is organized actively in ways that conform to our social needs and, as Ross and McFarland (1988) have argued, it is often recalled in a way that is biased to be consistent with what we are presently doing, thinking, or believing. For example, Miell (1987) showed that the present state of a relationship influences our memory for its original development, with the recent history of the relationship tending to color a person's recall of the more distant history of the relationship, such that pleasant recent experiences cause a rosy glow to suffuse the rest of the history while recent turbulence creates a more negatively loaded recall of the rest of the relationship. When breaking off relationships we may be more likely to remember the negative side of the relationship and to de-emphasize the positive if we are keen to get out, but we may cling to the positive and de-emphasize the negative if we hope desperately to stay in (Harvey et al. 1986). Memory for social experience thus serves a constructive purpose in shaping our relational lives (Duck and Sants 1983; Edwards and Middleton 1988) – not only in obvious cases (where, for example, we swear never to make the same mistake in a relationship ever again and so structure our relational behavior in ways calculated to avoid the same cycle) but also in other ways, as when partners reminisce as a way of reminding each other of the strength of a relationship and its significance to both of them (Duck 1985). Indeed, Edwards and Middleton (1988) have shown that parents use photograph albums to help children reminisce about their early years and use that time for emphasizing the role of others in the family, identifying key members of the group, re-emphasizing family ties, and so forth.

In short, we have to conclude that friendship and relationships do not involve special sorts of behavior but are embedded and "situated" in our ordinary lives (Ginsburg 1988 reviews this claim more thoroughly than space permits here). We continue as functioning human beings even in social situations or when we form friendships, and we take our human concerns and our regular styles of thinking, planning, and behaving into our relationships.

Exterior factors

Human life has a structure that comes not only from the cognitions, plans, projects, and concerns of its participants but also from the social context in which we are embedded. All of us are inevitably included in a human structure, a society, a civilization, a network of other people, a language system with its terminology and implications for describing friendship, a rule system indicating how to behave in certain circumstances (e.g. toward friends as distinct from neighbors) and so forth (G. J. McCall 1982). It is not possible to work, learn, eat, stay healthy, or do much else without other people, even if we wanted to. This social fact has two sides to it. As Morgan (1986) indicates, the sources from which one acquires the raw information that guides our daily life pose one question; the issue of how one acquires the resources to organize that information into usable knowledge is another. So we not only learn "facts" or norms from associating with other people, but also learn how to use and interpret those facts and to operate on them to translate them into socially acceptable behaviors. Our societal life necessitates our doing certain things, like talking to other people, and shapes our behavior in appropriate ways, exposes us to certain experiences, and makes us share societal concerns and attitudes in ways that impinge on and influence our formation, maintenance, and termination of relationships: for instance, we are often concerned about "what the neighbors or our parents will think" when we enter or dissolve relationships with particular people.

Cultural context

Our location in a culture presents us with particular styles and types of acceptable relationships that may be quite different from those acceptable and familiar in other cultures. For instance, those of us who inhabit western cultures would not normally consider entering arranged marriages or marriages where we did not love our partner (Simpson *et al.* 1986; but compare the findings of Kephart 1967 who found that over two-thirds of women then surveyed said that they would marry a man they did not love if everything else were satisfactory). Yet there are many cultures where arranged marriages are gladly entered into, and are considered to be perfectly normal, natural relationships that are anticipated with pleasure. Neither way of marrying is "right" or "wrong": they are just different.

There are other examples of our cultural or societal membership exposing us to "proper" ways to conduct relationships. For instance, the media in our culture expose us to certain representations of relationships. Soap operas and popular magazines alike display certain kinds of relationships between people, give us examples of how these relationships may be conducted, and can even serve as models for the course and content of the relationships in our own lives. Livingstone (1987) has recently reported a study in which she explored viewers' representations of the characters and relationships in the television soap opera *Dallas*, using Multi-Dimensional Scaling techniques. A major dimension that characterized viewers' perceptions of the characters was morality, while warmth and family values were closely associated. Livingstone's work also seems to suggest that viewers acquire a certain belief system associated with sex-roles (feminine ones being represented as family- and relationship-oriented, while the male ones are perceived as based on power and business acumen).

In an early consideration of the influence of media on our perception of relationships, Kidd (1975) examined popular magazines of the 1950s, 1960s, and 1970s and researched the sort of advice given about relationships. The typical style in the 1950s was one based on the implicit assumption that there is a single right or wrong way to conduct relationships and that people with problems could be given specific and universally applicable advice on how to act in them. For instance, it was claimed that "a man can feel kinship with the gods if his wife can make him believe he can cause a flowering within her" so the "worthiest duplicity on earth" was for a woman to fake orgasms (Kidd 1975)! Further, readers of such magazines were regularly presented with problem scenarios such as "What is this husband doing wrong?", "How can this marriage be saved?", "Where must a man have feminine traits?", and "What does a wife's paycheck do to her marriage?" In such cases the outline of the problem would be presented and the readers asked to judge the correct solution. A panel of experts would then provide the "correct answer" and point out a few major steps that should be taken. The notion was that there could be a correct solution for all problems, irrespective of the individuals concerned.

By contrast in the late 1960s, the same magazines were suggesting that the appropriate ways to solve relationship difficulties involved the couple's negotiating its own solution to its own problem, communicating with each other, and openly expressing their feelings and emotions, rather than concealing them or – worse – faking them. In these later views, universal rules for solving relational problems were not endorsed (except for the notion that "open communication is always good").

In addition to the ideas that we may assimilate by reading magazines, many indications about relationships are available from television. For instance, many people model their own behavior on the actions of players in soap operas, not only adopting their mannerisms but even taking on their styles of conducting relationships. A. M. Rubin *et al.* (1985) examined the possibility that lonely people might watch television in order to find out more about the proper way to conduct relationships, but found that lonely people watch more news programs and fewer "soaps" than do non-lonely persons. However, recent work has shown that such lonely persons have parasocial interaction with newscasters: they greet the newscaster, respond to sign-off comments, argue volubly with points made by the commentators, and even refuse to undress in the bedroom if the TV is on and a newscaster is talking to them! Research by Cortez (1986) showed that some newscasters get letters asking for advice on the best color to paint the viewer's living-room, or reporting that the viewer will be going on holiday shortly and that the newscaster should not feel offended if the viewer is not watching during that week. It has also been shown that newscasters are preferred if they are slightly humorous and acknowledge and address other members of the team (Horton and Wohl 1956). Clearly, then, we obtain information about relationships from the media, and in some cases use media personalities as substitutes for "real" friends.

Networks and the relationship of relationships

Such exterior cultural influences are important in themselves but so too are the influences that we derive from groups and our membership of them. Our lives are lived in communities and communities influence their members (Wellman 1985) both directly by the making of rules and laws (for example about who may marry whom) and indirectly through the social pressures inherent in our social interconnectedness with other people and the rules and norms for behavior in various relational settings. Thus, our moral behavior is likely to be influenced by our concerns over other people's reactions to what we do and groups maintain these influences by such means as gossip and intervention in relationships (LaGaipa 1982).

In addition, our relationships do not happen in a vacuum and often have their origins created or their limits set in other relationships. Parks and Adelman (1983) and Adelman (1987) have shown that lovers are often introduced by matchmakers or mutual friends. Also, our involvement in some relationships affects other relationships of ours (for example, when we marry a person of our choice, we automatically become sons- or daughters-in-law to specific people over whom we had no choice and vice versa: they are our in-laws because of their pre-existing relationship with our spouse). Dunn (1988) also shows how experience in some relationships early in life influences our perception of other relationships later in life. Finally, as Romeo and Juliet found dramatically, our membership of a particular group, family, or gang can restrict our freedom of choice among other relationships: if you were a Montague you could not marry a Capulet, however strong the mutual attraction. In sum, then, our membership in some relationships has mutual impact on other relationships in which we find ourselves; the circle of our acquaintances affects our opportunities to meet others, the range of knowledge to which we are exposed, our views of acceptability for certain types of behavior and our own evaluation of ourselves.

Other factors

A final human element that influences relationships and our conduct of them as ordinary human beings is that they are affected by the influences that in turn affect us during the life-cycle (Dickens and Perlman 1981). For one thing, this means that they are placed in a time frame; and our immediate concerns for relationships change and develop as time passes. The relationship needs of a newly married couple are different from those of a couple who have just had a first baby, which in turn differ from those of a couple whose youngest child has just left home (Dickens and Perlman 1981). For example, 30-year-old males seek more same-sex friendship patterns based on the work-place, while 20-year-old males are more actively seeking cross-sex relationships outside the work-place (Reisman 1981). These exterior influences of the life-cycle can direct and affect our relationships and our relationship choices.

Other relevant categories of influence on relationships and the behaviors that we display in them are such factors as personal skills in social context, the shy differing markedly from the non-shy not only in styles of relational performance but also in terms of attracting other people in the first place. We cannot assume safely that all persons seek or accomplish friendships in the same way, or that everyone has equivalent needs or skills. These differences need to be explored (see Chapters 2 and 3 for further consideration of this point).

Chance and coincidence also play a much underrated role in friendship and social relationships (Perlman 1986), since many "perfect partners" just find that one lives in Bismarck, North Dakota and the other in Tel Aviv, Israel. Similarly the "ideal" person whom we meet and fall in love with on vacation may well be unable to join us when we return home.

Summary and implications for the rest of the book

I have tried to show that "Relating to Others" is a much broader topic than it first appears to be. Although it used to be so conceived, it is not now restricted to such issues as why we like someone else; nor even is it encompassed by the traditional social psychological examination of those factors that lead to our feeling initially attracted to another person. New research in this domain concerns the questions of how to manage and maintain formed relationships, how to develop them, and how to cope with relationship decline. A full understanding of these issues would involve us in comprehending the contribution of many research disciplines other than psychology, but if one restricts oneself predominantly to social psychology, that too creates a broader enterprise than has previously been conceived. For example, it takes us into many more areas of social psychology than the obvious and historically well-researched ones and points us towards more specialized and advanced questions about familiar topics or incorporates them differently. For instance, development and application of research in other areas of social psychology might lead us to use the principles uncovered in research on interpersonal persuasion (investigating not how to change "big" attitudes about nuclear war or smoking, but how to persuade a partner to "get serious," for instance), attitude change ("how to make an enemy like us," for example), and attribution theory ("how to help someone understand why a partner left them," or "the role of accounts for first encounters in creating the sense of being in a relationship," for instance). The issue of the role of personality in friendship takes us further afield, to address questions such as how two personalities "match up" to make relationships work. Finally, examining some of the influences of friendship systems and social networks and the question of how social support helps us to survive crises takes us almost into sociology. We could explore the rules of behavior in relationships or the communication patterns that differentiate talk between friends from talk between strangers and that takes us into the social psychology of language or into communication science.

I have also tried to show that recent approaches to the above topics are centrally concerned with the development of new methodology for studying the advanced subject matter. As Kenny (1988) has cogently argued, research on relationships has previously been guided more by the available methods and analyses, to which our originally interesting questions were made to conform, rather than being guided by the interesting questions, for which new methods and analyses would have to be developed. As the rest of the book will show, a new style of work is now characteristic of this equally new field.

The study of friendship and relationships, far from being a small and narrow topic focused on attraction to strangers – as the research area used to be conceived – actually uses and cuts through much of social psychology, sociology, family studies, and interpersonal communication. We could employ almost all of the research in those disciplines to enhance our understanding of human relationships; equally we could use much of the new research on human relationships to enrich our understanding of social psychology more generally (Duck and Perlman 1985). After all, what is the basis of social behavior and interpersonal communication if it is not relationships with other people (as I have more fully argued in Duck 1986), and what is the source of human happiness and misery if it is not to be found in our friendships and social relationships? You may recall that it was with precisely this issue that the chapter began.

Further reading

Argyle, M. and Henderson, M. (1985). *The Anatomy of Relationships*. London: Methuen. An account of the nature of relationships, with a focus on the skills of relating and the rules that govern our behavior in relationships.

Derlega, V. J. (ed.) (1984). *Communication, Intimacy, and Close Relationships*. New York: Academic Press. This is a collection of papers on theories of relationships and how they operate. Chapters deal with such topics as self-disclosure, identity, and social control in relationships. The book is also a good source for general reading about this field.

Duck, S. W. (1986). *Human Relationships: An Introduction to Social Psychology*. London: Sage. This is a supplementary textbook designed to fill out the gaps in standard social psychology textbooks, which typically do not devote enough attention to human relationships. It presents research on emotions, non-verbal behavior, and verbal communication in developing the point that relationships underpin most social behavior. It contains other chapters on persuasion, social psychology and health, and on family relationships.

Duck, S. W. (ed.) (sections edited by S. W. Duck, D. F. Hay, S. E. Hobfoll, W. Ickes, and B. M. Montgomery) (1988). *Handbook of Personal Relationships*. Chichester: Wiley. This is the first and only handbook of research in personal relationships. It contains some thirty chapters, covering such research areas as communication, community and clinical psychology, developmental psychology, social psychology, and conceptualizations and methodology in the field.

Duck, S. W. and Gilmour, R. (eds) (1981). *Personal Relationships 1: Studying Personal Relationships*. London: Academic Press. This is a collection of theoretical papers on the nature of personal relationships and their study. Chapters deal with such topics as the best methods for studying relationships, the social context of relationships, exchange and equity in relationships, and sexual relationships.

Hinde, R. A. (1979). *Towards Understanding Relationships*. London: Academic Press. The book from which most people date the origin of the field of personal relationships. A classic account of the nature of relationships and of our needs in its study.

Huston, T. L. and Levinger, G. (1978). Interpersonal attraction and relationships. In M. R. Rosenzweig and L. W. Porter (eds) *Annual Review of Psychology*, vol. 29. Palo Alto, CA: Annual Reviews. An influential review of the state of play in the mid-1970s, which makes a number of important proposals for the development of the field.

Kelley, H. H., Berscheid, E., Christensen, A., Harvey, J. H., Huston, T. L., Levinger, G., McClintock, E., Peplau, L. A. and Peterson, D. R. (1983). *Close Relationships*. New York: Freeman. A book by nine leading scholars from the field of close relationships.

Peplau, L. A. and Perlman, D. (eds) (1982). *Loneliness*. New York: Wiley. The classic sourcebook for research on loneliness, which did more than anything to make the topic scientifically respectable. An excellent bibliography of research in loneliness is another of its outstanding features.

Weiss, R. S. (1974). The provisions of social relationships. In Z. Rubin (ed.) *Doing Unto Others*. Englewood Cliffs, NJ: Prentice-Hall. A classic statement of the needs that propel people into relationships and the resources and rewards that others provide for us in personal relationships.

2 / MEETING STRANGERS

There are many ways of relating to others: we may be kin to some, casual acquaintances of others, close friends of some, the marital partner or steady date of one, the father/daughter/mother/son/ sibling of others, and the working colleague of a few. Researchers have looked at relationships between work-mates (including romantic relationships in the work-place: Dillard and Miller 1988), at relationships between cooperative neighbors (O'Connell 1984), relationships between prisoners and guards (Hepburn and Crepin 1984), parents and children (C. N. Lewis and O'Brien 1987), children relating to other children (T. Adler and Furman 1988), siblings (Dunn and Kendrick 1982), and kin (Fitzpatrick and Badzinski 1985), to say nothing of the vast literature on the family. These cannot all be covered here in the available space and I will focus on voluntary intimate relationships, often those with a hint of romance.

Even so, there is growing work on the differences between types of such voluntary intimate relationships. For example K. E. Davis and Todd (1985) report on a procedure for classifying personal relationships according to the prototypes or "paradigm case formulations" that common folk – and other theorists – have for distinguishing between stages or types of relationships in the ideal case (for example the extent to which a particular relationship involves acceptance, trust, confiding, or support). Argyle and Henderson (1984; 1985a) use a rule system for classifying relationships; in other words they look at the rules that govern behavior in successful relationships of different types rather than at the ideal characteristics that people attribute to them. Thus they find that certain universal "maintenance" rules apply to all relationships (e.g.

respect other's privacy) and that special interpersonal reward rules apply to intimate relationships (e.g. express affection). Sternberg (1987), by contrast, develops not a typological or profile model of relationships, but a fundamental description of the dimensions of one type of relationship (love) that allows different kinds of that relationship to be distinguished, by reference to structural properties. For example if the basic emotion of love is created from the interaction of three structural elements (intimacy, passion, decision/commitment), different sorts of love can be understood in terms of the degree of each of these three elements that is present. Romantic love, for instance, comes from the combination of intimacy and passion, whereas infatuation comes from passion in the absence of intimacy or commitment (see Chapter 4 for more on love).

Such schemes for classifying and distinguishing relationships are important developments of earlier work (e.g. by Z. Rubin 1970, who first drew behavioral distinctions between liking and loving). While such work will undoubtedly develop vigorously in the 1990s, the discussion below centers on the general and common elements that human beings take into almost all of our relating to others and how we turn meetings with strangers (one type of relationship) into close friendship (another type).

However many types of relationships there may be, they all start in this same way – as a meeting between strangers. This is even, in some sense, true for parent–child relationships, but I will focus here mostly on friendships. A task for researchers has been to discover why it is that some pairs become friends while numerous other first meetings do not develop into friendships. (Interestingly, as Delia 1980 pointed out at length, researchers have typically focused much less on the equally interesting fact that most meetings do *not* develop into intimate relationships and that the trajectory for most relationships is to non-intimacy. But that, while an intriguing observation, is by the way and remains for future research to explore). Clearly we somehow select our friends from the range of people that we meet – and so the real question for us here, then, is how and why do we choose to develop relationships with some people and not others? What makes us feel attracted to some strangers but not others and, conversely, what makes us attractive to them?

By means of the mechanisms outlined in Chapter 1, some choices are taken for us by the pre-selecting that circumstances and society do for us to reduce the "field of availables" (Kerckhoff 1974): that is to say, the range or field of people that are *really* available for us to meet, rather than those that are theoretically available or theoretically eligible candidates for a relationship with us. There is considerable preselection, in any culture, of the types of people that we meet or become aware of (Woll and Cozby 1987) or tend to "regard" or treat as realistic possibilities for relationships (Rodin 1982). As noted in Chapter 1, they are mostly from our own race, religion, socioeconomic group, intelligence level, and educational background, and for various reasons those are also the people that we find most initially attractive as a group. (One reason is that similarity of such things makes communication easier since we share common assumptions; another reason is that similarity is simply reassuring). So our own personal choice has little to do with attraction at that point. Equally we are more likely to be interested in being attracted to other people in some circumstances rather than others; for example we are more "affiliative" and inclined to seek others' company when we are anxious (Schachter 1959), when we have just left a close relationship or moved to a new neighborhood (Duck 1982a), when aged between about 16 and about 26, when we are not in a hurry (Perlman 1986), and so on. Although face-to-face meetings will be the focus of discussion here, do not overlook the fact that they are by no means necessary preliminaries to acquainting nor the only way in which we become aware of others. Some other means are used by people who face barriers to initiation of relationships (Woll and Cozby 1987) such as shyness, lack of access to suitable pools of others (for example because of living in a very small town or working alone), lack of time, stigmata (like handicaps or overweight), or special needs (such as alternative life-styles). To meet such needs, as will be reported in more detail below, there is a growth in the use of personal ads or video-dating techniques for constructing meetings and bringing people together (Woll and Cozby 1987). These are modern-day technological equivalents of the introduction by means of visiting cards and third parties that were customary a hundred years ago, although even today some 60 per cent of students' dates are the result of introduction through mutual acquaintances (Duck and Cortez in preparation). By all of these means, both obvious and non-obvious, technological and basic, social and personal, our freedom of choice may be reduced from the theoretical maximum.

Given such, often unrealized or unnoticed, constraints on our choices, why are we attracted to certain others from among the whole field of "availables" that we meet? What makes them specifically members of the much smaller field of "desirables" or people we want to get to know? In the popular culture, there are several dozen different and competing answers to such questions, ranging from "dress for success" through "opposites attract" and "birds of a feather flock together" to "beauty is only skin deep" and "it's not what you say but the way that you say it." Each of us probably cherishes a different type of answer to the question. These are issues that have concerned the human species for thousands of years, and ever since people came to believe that we actually have a measure of free choice over the friendships that we make, there have been plenty of other people ready to offer advice on how to do it effectively. One of the world's most popular books was *How to Win Friends and Influence People* (Carnegie 1936) and the fact that this was a best-seller tells us something about the importance of the topic to a great number of people in many different countries and cultures. For all that common sense regards friendship as natural, it simply is not something that we really assume will happen "naturally" or unconsciously, nor is it something that we believe we cannot influence or help along by taking appropriate action. (One important issue that we shall return to later is the extent to which we think about relationships and how conscious thought affects relationships with others).

What does make us attractive to other people and what psychological principles explain attraction to strangers? A large amount of popular theorizing, many articles in popular magazines, hundreds of column-inches in advice columns, and the analyses of novelists, film-makers, and playwrights all preceded the development of industrious scientific research into these issues. If we take a while to look at some of the apparently "obvious" answers that have been produced by these means, we shall see why the question is still being asked: because it has not yet been satisfactorily answered by any of these people. The average person in the street can still sit and wonder about the causes of attractiveness.

Is beauty only skin deep?

One possible cause of attraction is physical appearance, and, using a variety of methods and techniques, researchers have vigorously studied its effects. For instance, we know that physically attractive people are preferred, to a degree (Dion *et al.* 1972), the "degree" being created largely by the match between our own physical attractiveness and the target's: if I think that the Other is "*too attractive for me*", I am less likely to try to enter a relationship unless I have lots of some resource other than physical attractiveness (such as money, power, or status). Murstein (1977) shows that dating partners select others who are of roughly equivalent physical attractiveness, as judged by outsiders, though Stroebe (1977) indicated that our own level of self-esteem about our physical attractiveness is also very important. In other words, Stroebe claims, indirectly, that two individuals will match on what *they think* their physical attractiveness is like, rather than on how it appears to other people. Snyder and Smith (1986) suggest that physical attractiveness is more important to some people than to others; more specifically, "high self-monitors" (who tend to be very aware of their own performance in social situations) consider physical attractiveness to be important, whereas "low self-monitors" (who tend to act as they like without always wondering what impression they are making) are more interested in others' internal qualities than in physical attractiveness. There is also the suspicion that physical attractiveness is not an unqualified positive asset, in that it seems likely to increase a partner's jealousy and hence to increase the inherent instability in a relationship (Bush *et al.* 1988). Furthermore, Krebs and Adinolfi (1975) indicated that those who are most physically attractive are more likely than physically unattractive persons to be rejected by the members of their own sex.

Thus the idea that beauty has a positive effect on relationships with other people is only partly supported by such research. However, it is very important to assess the sources from which the research flows and to evaluate the kinds of methods that have to be used to test the idea in the first place. I will therefore present a brief review of some of the main methods of conducting the research and we can then bear in mind during the reports of findings the somewhat tenuous methodology upon which those findings are based.

In much of the research on the topic it is important to realize that the assessments of physical attractiveness are based on photographs, which have been pre-rated by independent observers. Thus a typical style of research (e.g. Dion *et al.* 1972) would involve the presentation of a range of photographs to a group of raters. The most highly and most lowly rated pictures would then be used in an experimental manipulation (for example they may be attached to stories about children's behavior in order to see if the attractiveness of the child who is allegedly involved in the story has any effect on readers' assessments of the child's behavior). In a variation on this theme, Moore *et al.* (1987) showed slides of child and adult targets extensively pre-tested for physical attractiveness in order to study the ratings of overall target social desirability and of targets' alleged transgressions that would be produced by androgynous and sex-role-typed observers. They found that both sex-role-typed and androgynous observers reacted to physical attractiveness stereotypes and attributed more positive characteristics to the attractive targets. However, the androgynous observers did not go on to attribute lesser ratings of severity to the alleged transgressions of attractive children in the way that sex-role-typed observers did.

Another style of research, often where experimenters' confederates are used to lead other subjects on, involves making-up or dressing up a particular individual to be attractive or unattractive. In such cases (e.g. Walster *et al.* 1966) writers merely report that the target person was attractive or unattractive and describe the style of clothing that was worn or the make-up that was used to create the desired effect. In a more dramatic study, Dutton and Aron (1974) had a good-looking confederate female approach male subjects who had just walked across either the Capilano Suspension Bridge (a long, narrow, high, swaying, and thus anxiety-provoking bridge) or across a low and stable bridge (thought not to cause anxiety). During the course of the conversation, the confederate gave the men her telephone number. Nine out of thirty-three "highly anxious" subjects took up the opportunity to call the female after the experiment, while only two of the "low anxiety" subjects did – a result usually interpreted to show that anxiety, or any strong arousal, can increase attraction to a willing, physically attractive person.

Since one method involves the interaction of a subject with a living human being, often one who promises or suggests a future dating possibility as part of the experimental manipulation, while the other involves merely the aesthetic appreciation of a still photograph, it is likely that judgements and relationship consequences are rather different in the two methodological cases. However, Riggio and Woll (1984) have shown that videotapes of possible dating partners are rather informative to clients at a video-dating agency, so we may actually be influenced by the same cues whether or not we interact with the target person. Woll and Cozby (1987) have indicated that videotapes supply clients with "a wide variety of indepth, naturalistic information about prospective dates [and so] enable these clients to make more informed, more rational choices than they would make under other circumstances". This argument is buttressed by the facts that videos can be repeatedly played, that the client is not "on the spot" himself or herself in an interaction, that the client knows the videotaped person has already decided to be available for dating, and that the client retains personal control over choices without the hassles or guilt about rejecting or being rejected face-to-face. On the other hand, such a method is available only to the financially independent and the research is in its early days, and thus is developing in quality all the time.

It is also worth noting that studies typically evaluate physical attractiveness by means of *facial* characteristics rather than other parts of the body, although some of the earliest systematic work on the topic of beauty (Perrin 1921) distinguished between static beauty (and, incidentally, included ratings of attractiveness based on nails and teeth) and dynamic beauty, in terms of "nice" behavior. There have nevertheless been studies where silhouettes of whole bodies were rated for attractiveness (e.g. Beck *et al.* 1976) from which it is found, for example, that women prefer (in those circumstances at least) men with prominent buttocks and large chests. A recent questionnaire survey of some American psychology students (Franzoi and Herzog 1987), however, found that body shape as a whole is relevant to both men's and women's ratings of physical attractiveness, with upper body shape being most important in judgements about men and overall weight being most important in judgements about women. In an impressive variation on this theme, Alicke *et al.* (1986) created composite slides from faces and bodies photographed during two summers at a swimming pool (the kind of scientific research job we would all like to have). They were able to create slides showing persons with attractive bodies and unattractive faces, the same attractive body but with an attractive face, and so on, by means of photographic processing techniques. Their study then proceeded by showing the slides to an audience of subjects who rated them. It was found that faces affected ratings of intelligence, sociability, and morality while bodies influenced ratings only of sociability and intelligence!

Given the previous remarks about the difficulty of investigating the question realistically, it nevertheless seems entirely probable, on first sight, that the more physically attractive members of the community will also be the more attractive socially, however unfair or unpalatable this may be (Berscheid 1981). Social desirability derives from physical attractiveness to a very large extent (Berscheid 1981).

Physically attractive people, as contrasted with physically unattractive people in experiments and studies of the types described above, are believed to be more sensitive, kind, interesting, strong, poised, modest, sensible, outgoing, exciting, and sexually warm and responsive persons (Berscheid 1981: 10). Studies by Dion *et al.* (1972) and Dion (1972), using stimulus photographs attached to stories, have shown collectively that physically attractive people are better liked and are rated more favorably on a number of important dimensions, ranging from intelligence to lack of mischievousness. In some of the studies in the Dion series, it was found that physically attractive children were rated as less disruptive and less dispositionally naughty than were unattractive children described as committing the same acts in the same circumstances. In other words, we are prepared to disregard naughtiness in children who are attractive and we are likely to think that they are not really naughty children; they arc just being impish on this particular occasion.

A great deal of research, then, confirms that we react more favorably to physically beautiful people than we do to less attractive, ugly, or deformed people. However, we need to think about this more, based as the evidence is on studies which use photographs rather than face-to-face interaction, and which do so in the short term ("How do you react to this photograph? . . . OK, now you can go") rather than the long-term series of encounters that make up everyday interactions and relationships. Of course *unattractive* people have friendships, go on dates, get married, become parents, succeed at work, become concert pianists, win Cordons Bleus and awards for outstanding research, climb Mount Everest, become airline pilots, and so on. Equally some beautiful-looking people are social outcasts, since our stereotypes often include the notions that beauty and brains are negatively correlated and that the *very* attractive are also egocentric, spoiled, and hatefully rich! Work by Reis *et al.* (1980) indicates that level of physical attractiveness makes only some (very small) difference to the rates of social participation of the relevant individuals, and that these differences are not what we might expect. Physically attractive men have more interactions than do less attractive men, but physically attractive women do not seem to have more social interaction than less attractive ones. Attractive people of either sex have more satisfying interactions; at least, they report being more satisfied with their interactions.

It seems likely, then, that physical attractiveness affects the choices that people make of one another, or the ratings that we make about other persons, but rating another person as attractive is hardly the basis for a relationship. We would probably like to think that physical attractiveness has no effect beyond the initial steps. Indeed, thus far I have not shown that it affects the success or progress of long-term relationships.

To accept that beauty creates long-term success in relationships, even if it does increase a person's social opportunities, is neither very appealing nor completely accurate. Many people react negatively to beautiful people, envying them or resenting them or fearing to approach and invite them into relationships because it is assumed that they are involved in lots of satisfying relationships already or that they have higher standards and will be more rejecting. This belief seems to be unjustified in reality, however, for Reis *et al.* (1980) have shown that the level of a woman's physical attractiveness is not predictive of her level of social participation. Furthermore, as argued by Duck and Sants (1983), relationships are not created by the mere "chemistry of partner attributes", that is they do not spring into life from the mere mixing together of positively valued social attributes, such as physical beauty or an attractive personality. Relating to others involves interaction and social processes that can override the effects of initially positive responses to superficial characteristics of immediate aesthetic reactions to external appearance. What physical attractiveness may do, however, is influence the range of persons who regard themselves as available to us and there is research suggesting (however undesirable the fact is) the relative importance to women of their own physical attractiveness, in both the short and the long term (Freedman 1986). However, other research shows that in longer-term real-life relationships, physical attractiveness seems to have a greater effect on men's relationships than on women's (Reis *et al.* 1980). The research taken as a whole seems to show that it works mostly at the point of expressing preferences, in the case of date selection in a laboratory study. Neither is the (assumed) effect of attractiveness on long-term relationships fully supported by other parts of common sense: most people seem to believe that physical attraction is only a little relevant to our choices of friendships and dating partners, but that, beyond that, it is personality and attitudes that account for success, stability, companionship, and depth in relationships. If this is not the case, human beings are disappointingly shallow.

Looking beneath the surface

Most of us assume that there is more to life and relationships than physical attractiveness; we tend to think, for instance, that rich and successful people or highly intelligent ones will be more attractive than their opposites, whether or not they are physically attractive. Most social psychological research assumes that the whole panoply of a person's attributes, reward value, and negative qualities will be brought to bear on the assessment of their ultimate social value and worth, even if attributes such as physical appearance are mentioned and attended to more often at the dating stage.

In some intriguing work on the advertisements that people place in the personal columns of newspapers, several researchers have examined the kinds of "advantages" that advertisers proclaim themselves to have in the partnership stakes. As Lynn and Bolig (1985) have noted, this means of meeting partners is increasingly respectable and more frequently used nowadays than it once was, but we should note that this is particularly true of middle-class, white "yuppies" and that research on this topic, having only recently begun, has some way to go before it reaches the peaks of quality.

Cameron *et al.* (1977) and Harrison and Saeed (1977) investigated the kinds of statements made by men and women who placed ads. Their research questions were: what do advertisers note as their best "selling points"? Are men and women likely to advertise the same sorts of advantages? Cameron *et al.* (1977) found a remarkable tendency for advertisers' claims and requests to conform to traditional role expectations then in force: that is men tended to stress status as an attractive characteristic, while women mentioned their appearance more often. Harrison and Saeed (1977) found that women were very likely to seek financial security, to stress the need for sincerity and genuineness in replies, and to ask for dates with men older than themselves. Men usually asked for attractive partners who were younger than themselves and who were looking for a long-term relationship such as marriage. More recent work reported in Lynn and Bolig (1985) indicates that women made more references to the personality traits, education, and careers of themselves and their prospective partner, while men mentioned physical appearance and interests or activities that they enjoyed. As we shall see in more detail in Chapter 4, it is usual for men to see intimacy in terms of joint activities and interests, and for women to see it more in terms of emotional confiding (Hendrick 1988 provides a substantial review of this work). These findings are therefore quite consistent with this established sex difference.

In the market-place for setting up meetings with strangers, personal advertisers clearly support the common beliefs that certain features of themselves are more relevant to attraction than others and these are basically predictable from the traditional norms held in a society about the characteristics of "men" and "women." Hendrick (1988) regards the particular traits of "masculinity" and "femininity" (or "androgyny," a mixture of the two) as self-ascribed qualities that are functional for the initiation of relationships, making it feel to the individual that it is either "appropriate" or "inappropriate" to take the initiative in relating or to "offer" certain properties or qualities in relationships. Thus it would be likely that men who feel that they are "masculine" and women who feel that they are "feminine" would be more likely than androgynous individuals to advertise themselves in terms conforming to sex stereotypes and would be less likely to mention characteristics atypical of their ascribed sex; for example we might predict that they would be likely to mention their appearance if they happen to conform to the male–female stereotype physically. Indeed, recent work by Koestner and Wheeler (1988) indicates that, at least in personal ads, the two sexes tend to "offer" the attributes that popular culture suggests will be attractive to the other sex. Women "offer" slimness and physical attractiveness and "seek" taller men, for instance, while men "seek" women who are slim and shorter than themselves, while they "offer" their own height and social status in such ads.

Such a conclusion is a rather depressing reflection on human judgements and priorities. Are such things as outward appearance, wealth, status, and age more important to most people than personal qualities? We should recognize the special nature of the situation in personal ads, though, since advertisers have to present their positive side in a way that is both easy to assimilate and economical in terms of space. It is very likely that they will fall back on traditionally acceptable themes to emphasize their "normality" and will then put in one or two individualizing thoughts only toward the end, if at all. As we have all learned to our cost, the enticing descriptions of other "goods" in advertisements can be misleading when it comes to the sustained enjoyment of them in the realities of their long-term performance capacities. We can soon find that beautiful chrome-plating is less important than the fact that the character of the device does not suit our needs in everyday use. It may be more likely that personality characteristics and attitudes – the depth of a person's humanity – are the real key to success in attracting strangers into relationships. How well does that idea work as an explanation of attraction?

Beyond the outer limits

One possible way to explain initial attraction would be to attend to the personality that an individual brings to relationships with others and/or to examine its "objective attractiveness." A separate issue, to be considered later in the chapter, is how an individual's personality affects his or her behavior in relationships, while yet another set of questions are concerned with the degree to which the "fit" between two personalities affects the quality of a long-term relationship between individuals. Having noted that these questions arise as research issues in their own right, at this point we are looking only at one personality and how its likability is rated.

Some types of personalities are thought to be more attractive than others. For example our culture values outgoing sociability rather than shyness, and for this reason extraversion is regarded more favorably than introversion. Thus extraverted strangers are rated as more attractive partners than introverted ones (Hendrick and Brown 1971). This is a general judgement of extravert/introvert personalities made by observers who have not interacted with the specific person and it is based only on the reading of some personality scales completed by the individual: a strictly one-sided set of circumstances. The procedure here is comparable to showing a person a photograph of someone else and asking what the viewer thinks – and just as misleading. Nevertheless we should bear in mind that on first encounter we are unable to process the "depth" of someone's personality and so we have to focus on surface attributes. Thus extraverts are likely to be rated as more attractive than introverts if we take simple measures of initial attraction. If we explore the issue more thoroughly, though, we find that such general descriptions of a person become less important as an acquaintanceship proceeds (Duck 1977a). Partners will undoubtedly be more concerned with the depth of one another's personality structure and attitudes. They will also start to consider the ways in which partners' personalities and attitude structures match up (Duck and Craig 1978): whether or not the partners are similar, for example, or whether the two of them get along, regardless of the type of personality that each has.

Attitudes

The idea that similarity of attitudes might create positive feelings in partners is an appealing one and we might initially feel that our partners are probably rather similar to ourselves in attitudes. Obviously we like others to be somewhat similar to ourselves, although few of us would want our friends to be cardboard replicas of ourselves. What is often (somewhat inaccurately) known as "the similarity hypothesis" thus starts from the position that such similarity is likely to be generally attractive and that attitude similarity will be particularly attractive to us because it represents specific similarity of thinking – and that is always rewarding.

Even if we agree that attitude similarity is likely to be important in attraction to other people, there are a number of immediate problems in approaching the question from a research point of view. First, the fact that friends seem to us to be similar in attitudes does not tell us very much. Quite apart from the fact that our perceptions may be inaccurate and we may *see* friends as being more similar to us than they really are, the mere existence of similarity does not tell us why it exists. Were our friends similar to us to start with, causing us to like them? Or did we originally like them for other reasons and then the similarities increased between us as the friendship progressed? That problem is a critical one if we are to establish the direction of causality and thereby learn whether similarity causes attraction or attraction causes similarity. (In fact, both T. Newcomb 1961 and Blankenship *et al.* 1984 have shown in different ways that both are true simultaneously). Another issue concerns the time at which similarity exerts an influence on the course of an acquaintance: perhaps similarity matters at some points and not others (physical attractiveness may be more important in first encounters and attitude similarity might become important later on). Perhaps similarity of different things matters at different points anyway (similarity of educational background could be important in bringing people together in the first place, but similarity of religious attitudes might be more important in keeping people together – Duck 1977a).

Let us begin with the issue of causality: does similarity cause attraction or result from it? Byrne (1961) provided a solution to this problem. To answer the question scientifically it is important to manipulate the level of similarity between two people and then measure the level of attraction between them. But how do you manipulate the level of similarity between people? Either they are

similar or they are not – or so it seems. Byrne solved this problem by
creating a paradigm for research that became known as "the bogus
stranger" method. The essence of this procedure is that subjects first
arrived in the laboratory and were given an attitude questionnaire to
complete. At some point the completed questionnaire was collected
while the subject was given some other task to perform to keep him
or her occupied. At that point Byrne or one of his associates
completed another questionnaire so that the second one corre-
sponded to the subject's original questionnaire answers to some
given degree (say 20 or 50 or 80 per cent). This second questionnaire
was then returned to the subject along with some comments leading
the subject to believe that the form had been completed by another
subject who was sitting in a second laboratory (this non-existent
stranger is usually referred to as "the bogus stranger" after whom the
technique is named – although the true subject does not of course
know that the stranger is bogus). The subject was then asked to rate
"the stranger" on a set of scales measuring liking.

The idea is a simple but clever one: if liking is caused by similarity
of attitudes, the more attitude similarity that the experimenter
establishes between the subject and the bogus stranger, the more the
subject should rate the stranger as likable and attractive under these
conditions. The findings seem to bear out the idea: in a number of
studies it has been shown that generally the greater the similarity, the
greater the liking (Byrne 1969; 1971). If the attitudes are important
or unusual, the similarity is more significant and creates greater
impact (Byrne *et al.* 1966; Lea and Duck 1982). The subject has to
begin by seeing the stranger as a genuine person who is stating truly
held beliefs, who is not mentally disturbed, and who has no other
disqualifying stigmas (Byrne and Lamberth 1971). However, the
basic idea seems to work, despite the fact that some commentators
(e.g. Eiser 1980) find it repellent, while others (e.g. Gergen 1980)
regard it as a very superficial approach to the study of attraction.

Those commentators who criticize Byrne's approach for its arti-
ficiality seem to miss the point. The problem is not that the manipulation of similarity is unrealistic, for Byrne is interested in the effects of
manipulation of attitude similarity whether or not it is artificial. The
crucial omission from Byrne's work is the way in which we actually
detect similarity or judge it to exist in our real-life relationships
(Duck 1986). In Byrne's defence, however, we must note that it is not
his task alone to solve all scientific questions about similarity and
he clearly performed a service in establishing its significance in

attraction. Other researchers can now proceed from the base that he established to investigate the role of attitude similarity in a larger context.

In so far as attitudes are structured into a person's cognitions along with other elements and features, we can expect their primary role in attraction to be ceded to these other elements as time goes by, as has indeed been shown by Duck and Craig (1978). In their longitudinal study of real-life friendships it was found that some types of similarities related to friendship at some points in its development while others assumed significance at a later point. Specifically similarity of answers on a multi-question format inventory (the California Psychological Inventory, or CPI) mattered most at first encounters while similarity in the subjects' own terms and thought-values (personal constructs) mattered most at a later stage (several months later). As acquaintance develops, we obviously learn more subtle facts or features from our partner, just as he or she does from us. So we probably take more account of the grand and fine structure of his or her personality and how it meshes with our own (Duck 1973).

Personality

Most people would probably claim that one's personality is reflected in the ways one behaves, and it is our behavior that makes us attractive to other people. For instance Bell and Daly (1984) argue that, rather than just letting things happen, we quite consciously and deliberately try to make ourselves attractive by adopting certain kinds of special behavior in affiliative contexts when we are trying to attract other people. For instance we try to be polite, we try to indicate our trustworthiness, and we may even show our range of abilities and behaviors as far as possible (see Chapter 3 for a fuller account). In the interactions of everyday life, however, there are three components: how we feel about the other person's personality as a stimulus, and how they feel about ours as a stimulus (that is whether or not we like their personality and they like ours); how their personality style matches up with ours in theory (that is whether we like the way our two personalities work "as a team"); and how their personality influences their behavior – and how ours influences ours – to make the relationship more satisfying for us both (that is whether our personality-driven behaviors help us both to lead satisfactory, interconnected lives).

Early research focused on the ways in which two people were similar to one another in personality (Richardson 1939) and how that affected their relationship in the long or short term (Day 1961). As the work developed, researchers began to wonder whether this style of research was appropriate to the questions that concern initial attraction and they concluded that its proper place is in relation to the question of later development of the relationship where partners, in the normal processes of real life, will have begun to appreciate such aspects of one another (Duck 1977a). Much research was conducted on the role of similarity or oppositeness in personality, with the issue focusing on the relationship between the two independent personalities of the two independent people embarking on the relationship. It was as if we could predict how well two people would get on together, even though all we knew about them was what they were like as individuals who had not yet met. If you think about it, that is an interesting "westernized" version of the eastern idea that you can arrange marriages between people on the basis of knowledge about their incomes, social standing, and family – the only difference being the supposition that their personalities are what matter, not their family origins.

Indeed, dating agencies tell us that a good way to match ourselves up with partners for successful relationships is on the basis of our interests, our values, and our personality characteristics. The notion here is that we align ourselves with someone else who shares our concerns and our priorities or who holds the same kinds of values as we do. The implications are twofold: not only will we be more attracted (and attractive) to someone who shares our thought-styles in the first place, but also our relationship with them will also be more satisfying and successful in the long term. Thus the matching of our value systems will get us off to a good start and also keep us running smoothly as the relationship develops.

Others have taken the view that personality matching is the basis for relationships (Levinger and Breedlove 1966): that is to say that the match of personalities of two people (whether they are similar, for instance, or complementary opposites) underlies the selection and successful conduct of relationships. Such people typically think that the "true" personalities of people have to be matched up: that is scientists should take measures of the individuals' personalities and score them scientifically. That way we can see whether the two people are similar (or complementary) and we can predict their choices. Dating agencies believe this, too, on a less scientific level, and usually require clients to complete some form of personality inventory as part of their procedures.

There are several examples of good scientific work to test this notion, and also a few egregious examples of confusions that it generated (see Duck 1977a for a review). To summarize, some twenty-five years of research did little to resolve the issue clearly. The role of similarity of personality was not properly clarified because studies tended to compare relationships that are fundamentally different (e.g. marriage and same-sex friendship), to compare different points in the development of the relationship (e.g. initial contact and long-term courtship), and to use personality measures that have different purposes, functions, and concerns (e.g. value priorities versus extraversion–introversion assessments). Equally important, subtly but significantly different measures of similarity are often used by different investigators (e.g. similar total scores on a test, however that total was arrived at, versus exactly the same answers to specific questions: see Duck 1977a, Chapter 6, for a full discussion).

Such styles of research have now been developed as more sophisticated work has built on the previous contributions. For instance, Van Lear and Trujillo (1986) have shown that in the process of forming and maintaining impressions of a partner's personality a person will change focus as time passes. To start with, the person places greatest emphasis on reduction of general uncertainty and finding out what the other person's personality is like in a very broad way. This exercise then forms the basis for an exploration of the affective nature of the relationship as it develops. Partners begin to show greater concern over such issues as their feelings of ease develop, as their sense of caution reduces, and as their beliefs about being accepted by the other person grow. Evidently, once the person seems to be an acceptable person (as deduced from the first stage of the enterprise) we then start to be more interested in whether or not they like us and can hold a reasonably comfortable interchange with us. After that, we become interested in the issue of personal growth: partners make many more positive judgements about one another and express or indicate their interpersonal attraction in clearer and clearer ways. Intimacy increases and so does the enjoyment of one another's company. Finally the fourth stage, interpersonal stability, is characterized by a decline in most of the searching that characterizes the early stages, and the couple does not engage in such "driven" seeking of information and uncertainty reduction. In other words, the role of information about another person tends to

diminish as the acquaintance develops and the relative importance of
the "feel" or organization of the relationship becomes greater. To
put it another way, the affect that we feel towards a partner begins by
being based on information about them but soon moves to a base
founded on the behaviors and activities that we share.

[Perceived] Actions speak louder than [disembodied knowledge about] cognitions

To summarize the above, personality was originally viewed in this
context as information about someone else; the independent personalities of the two individuals were presumed to be matchable in
the absence of any information about their interaction together as
people (that is their success in relationships was viewed as predictable from knowledge of them as individual personalities); and the
different layers of personality were, at best, presumed to have
different relevance over the term of an acquaintanceship (Duck
1977a; Duck and Craig 1978), but usually they were not seen as
distinct nor was the distinction seen to matter very much.

Despite its currency, there are reasons for dissatisfaction with this
conceptualization of the issue. A major drawback is that it implies
that the "true" personality of the two relating partners, as assessed
by scientific tests, is what counts and that the actual behavior of the
partners in a real relationship has no significant impact on the course
or stability of their relationship, except in so far as it gives one person
information about the other's personality and thereby affects partners' willingness to remain together. I would much rather believe
something else (Duck 1977a; cf. Kelley *et al.* 1983): namely that the
actions we take in a relationship, whether we act fairly and kindly,
whether we help someone, whether we share our intimacies with
them – even whether we help with the dishes – make the difference to
the conduct of the relationship and to our feelings of belonging to the
partnership. It is not merely a question of our feelings toward a
disembodied personality inventory that shape our relationships; the
most significant role is played by our evaluation and experience of
the other person's reactions toward us. These reactions depend on
and are influenced by the long-term conduct of the relationship and
partners' attempts to make the relationships work.

Summary

In this chapter I have been trying to indicate the fundamental inadequacy of some common-sense assumptions about attraction to strangers. I have also tried to show the difficulty of conducting adequate scientific studies of some of the obvious issues in attraction, such as the role of physical attractiveness. We learned to be cautious about extrapolating from studies of photographs to statements about attraction in the cut and thrust of daily life. We also examined some of the answers that can be given to some central questions, on the basis of developing research. In order of importance, rather than order of appearance in the chapter, some conclusions about attraction are as follows:

1 Attraction is not the same as forming an acquaintance and different factors are influential at different stages in an acquaintanceship. The role of time in relationships is important and, as the book proceeds, the psychological and relational effects of time will be progressively delineated.
2 Knowledge about personality is not the same as the effects of personality on behavior. Although many studies were conducted on the basis of the matching of personality questionnaires, it is obvious that such questionnaires do not form the basis for the interpersonal communication that creates relationships in real life.
3 Relational behavior is not based solely on cognition: we perform social actions as well as think (about) them. A major part of creating a relationship is the coordination of social actions of the two individual partners, rather than their reactions, impressions, or thoughts about one another.
4 Cues for initial attraction are not necessarily the same as those that predict long-term happiness or relationship stability.
5 Organization of daily life is more important to our relationships than are attitudes alone.

The next chapter pursues these ideas in the context of relationship development.

Further reading

Alicke, M. D., Smith, R. H., and Klotz, M. L. (1986). Judgements of physical attractiveness: The role of faces and bodies. *Personality and Social*

Psychology Bulletin, 12, 381–9. An experimental report, briefly described in this chapter, assessing the relative importance of faces and body shape in overall judgements of attractiveness, along with a determination of the "meaning" of each.

Berscheid, E. (1985). Interpersonal attraction. In G. Lindzey and E. Aronson (eds) *Handbook of Social Psychology*, vol. 2, 3rd edn. New York: Random House. A review of work on attraction which also, despite its title, considers some of the new style of research described here.

Byrne, D. (1971). *The Attraction Paradigm*. New York: Academic Press. A rigorous account of Byrne's extensive research on attraction to strangers.

Derlega, V. J. and Winstead, B. A. (1986). *Friendship and Social Interaction*. New York: Springer-Verlag. This is a collection of chapters on the development and maintenance of friendship. It presents chapters on such topics as friendship in the work-place, sex-differences in same-sex friendship and approaches to friendship disorders. Of particular relevance to the present chapter are the papers by Winstead and Derlega; Perlman and Fehr; Berg and Clark; and Miell and Duck.

Duck, S. W. (1977). *The Study of Acquaintance*. Farnborough: Gower. An evaluative review of work on initial attraction and acquaintance including assessment of major difficulties in work on personality similarity, some of which still remain.

Duck, S. W. and Gilmour, R. (1981). *Personal Relationships 2: Developing Personal Relationships*. London: Academic Press. This volume deals with the development of relationships through time, whether from infancy to adulthood or "from strangers to lovers."

Duck, S. W. and Perlman, D. (eds) (1985). *Understanding Personal Relationships Research: An Interdisciplinary Approach*. London: Sage. This is an edited volume of papers on a whole range of issues covered by the most recent research in relationships, such as personal needs and relationships, the rules of relationships, and people's conceptual schemas for relationships. Particularly relevant to the issues in the present chapter are the papers by Davis and Todd; McAdams; Argyle and Henderson; and Wright.

Freedman, R. (1986). *Beauty Bound*. Lexington, MA: Gower. A book giving some important insights into the role of physical attractiveness in modern society.

Hendrick, C. and Hendrick, S. S. (1983). *Liking, Loving and Relating*. Monterey, CA: Brooks/Cole. A very useful account of experimental work on attraction, love, and some broader issues in the relationship field.

Huston, T. L. and Levinger, G. (1978) Interpersonal attraction and relationships. In M. R. Rosenzweig and L. W. Porter (eds) *Annual Review of Psychology*, vol. 29. Palo Alto, CA: Annual Reviews. An influential review of the state of play in the mid-1970s and making a number of important proposals for the development of the field.

3 / DEVELOPING A RELATIONSHIP

Developing a relationship might seem to be something that "just happens" once we start to feel positive about someone else. It feels as if it has an inevitability about it that is mostly to do with our increased liking for, and acquisition of knowledge about, our partners – and vice versa. The more the relationship develops, the more we get to know about our partner; conversely the more we get to know about them, the more the relationship develops. Another aspect of the development of a relationship is growth of intimacy, with greater feelings of relaxation, more bending of the "relationship rules," greater familiarity, greater physical intimacy, and greater psychological closeness. We also do things with partners that we do not do with other people: we choose to spend our time with them and we go to places with them.

It is commonly believed that the development of relationships is closely related to information acquisition or to uncertainty reduction. This notion is quite widespread and has been vigorously researched so I will discuss it in detail below. The most recent research has made it clear that there is much more to the development of relationships than that alone, however. In any case, even if information acquisition does have an important role in relationship development, we must not regard it as a simple passive process whereby information is somehow magically received by the two partners and has the unambiguous effect of promoting the relationship. In the past few years, researchers have arrived at a much clearer picture of the strategies, devices, and techniques that partners use to seek information, to encourage partners to provide it, to interpret it, to convey information about themselves actively to other people in strategic ways, and even to conceal it or strategically avoid topics that have the potential to ruin the relationship or prevent it from developing. Much research looks at friendship or at courtship. While the issues in the two cases are sometimes different, there are nevertheless common principles and I shall focus here on the similarities; however Chapter 4 will be devoted to the research that deals with courtship. You might also spot some differences in the *processes* on which the research focuses in the two cases.

What are we trying to develop when we develop a relationship?

It is difficult to define what develops when a relationship develops, since a lot of what happens is "all in the mind." People certainly change their lives in major or minor ways to accommodate the new relationship, but the "sense of being in the relationship" is what makes the real difference (Duck and Sants 1983) and couples often develop a story about where they first met (Duck and Pond 1988 – by the way, if you can think of any *new* jokes about this pair of authors, let me know). Such stories may be inaccurate or accurate, but that is less the point than is the fact that people regard the stories as meaningful and treat them *as if* they were true. It is partly the emergence of such stories that marks the time (often quite early on) when the partners realize that they are "in a relationship" rather than just being two people who have met one another on a number of occasions and talked and done things together. It is therefore necessary to consider what a relationship might be, so that we can begin to reach an understanding of how it comes to be.

According to Hinde (1981), the nature of relationships is determined by a set of features which change and intensify as the relationship proceeds. He argues that we can achieve some understanding of relationships by looking at where they are located on the following eight dimensions of assessment.

1 *Content of interactions.* Relationships derive much of their essence from the things that the partners do together: customer–waiter relationships differ from father–daughter relationships in the nature of the activities that occur within the relationship. For a father to charge his daughter for every meal or cup of coffee in the home, for instance, or for customer and waiter to hug and tell one

another secrets or play hide-and-seek would violate the norms for conducting their respective relationships. The types of activities typically engaged in help to define the relationship and differentiate it from others. Naturally, as relationships develop (from acquaintance to close friendship, for example) so the partners will alter their interactions to embrace different content. They may talk to one another about different subjects or go to different places: indeed it is sometimes a quite significant escalation of a relationship for one person to invite another to visit his or her home or to talk about a previously taboo area – a sign of the breaking of a barrier and an indication of a desire to increase the intimacy.

2 *Diversity of interactions.* Some relationships do not involve a lot of variety of action. Student–instructor relationships, for example, are typified by interactions concerned with tasks that are focused on a rather limited range of topics to do with the relevant academic discipline and do not normally involve going on picnics or talking about holiday travel plans. On the other hand, parent–child relationships involve a lot of diversity – playing, instructing, comforting, protecting, educating, healing, feeding, and so on. Hinde (1981), adopting a distinction current in sociology (e.g. Barnes 1972; Boissevain 1974), therefore draws a distinction between uniplex relationships (where the types of interactions are limited in scope) and multiplex relationships (where the varieties of interactions are far greater). One way to classify and differentiate relationships, therefore, is in terms of the diversity of interactions that comprise them: the more diverse the interactions, the deeper the relationship.

3 *Qualities of interactions.* Although the content of interactions is significant, the "adverbial properties" (Duck and Sants 1983) are important too: it's not what you do but the way that you do it. A significant means of understanding relationships, therefore, is in terms of the qualities of the interactions that occur. We can assess these qualities by examining the intensity and style of interactions, the non-verbal signals exchanged, and so on. Intensity could be measured simply – for example, by checking whether the partners shout at one another or whisper in each other's ear. Style could be assessed in terms of the "immediacy" of the language they use (Duck 1986; Mehrabian 1972; Norton 1983), for example, whether one person includes the other in the content of the speech (by saying "We went together," for instance, or "I went and X

came along," which convey different messages about the relationship between the speaker and X). Non-verbal signals are also important: they are the bodily cues that accompany speech in socially significant ways – such as whether we look directly at someone when we speak to them or look down sheepishly, or whether we smile or frown when they talk to us (Argyle 1983).

4 *Relative frequency and patterning of interactions.* One of the clearest signals of an increasingly deepening voluntary relationship is the increase in frequency of meetings between the persons. In the case of involuntary relationships, like close family ties, there are other and better indices of increasing closeness such as the affection expressed verbally and non-verbally, the absence of conflict, and so on. We meet people more often out of choice because we like to or we want to enjoy their company more often. Thus friends increase the frequency of meetings as their relationship grows (Hays 1988). Another signal is the way in which interactions are patterned according to societal norms or the preferences of partners: thus for a couple to make love more often than the social norm tells us something about their sense of duty to society's statistics, but does not tell us about their relationship or their sexual satisfaction unless we map it on to their expressed desires for sex. The answer to the question "How is their sexual activity patterned relative to the wishes of each partner?" could reveal much more information about the nature of the relationship between the partners than is revealed by simple statistics about the absolute frequency of their sexual activity. Thus Blumstein and Schwartz (1983) show that even in happily married couples, frequency of intercourse varies between "less than once per month" (about 6 per cent of couples happily married between two and ten years) to "three or more times per week" (about 27 per cent of couples happily married for more than two years).

5 *Reciprocity and complementarity.* In some relationships I do what you do. You say "How are you?", and I say "Fine, how are you?"; or you buy me a drink, and I feel obligated to buy you one. You invite me to dinner and I say "No, you took me out last time, now it's my turn." These are reciprocal actions and the sense of superficiality in a relationship is directly related to the degree to which you do feel obligated to reciprocate: the more superficial the relationship, the more people keep count of whose turn it is to

do the behavior next. On the other hand, when I ask you for help and you give it, or you try to dominate and I submit, or you look in need of a hug and I give you one, then our behavior is complementary: it is different behavior but it goes together to make a perfect whole. In complementary behaviors people take account of each other's needs to a greater extent, by definition. Thus relationships where reciprocity is greater than complementarity are on the whole less intimate (Berg and Clark 1986) and complementarity develops with the relationship.

6 *Intimacy.* There are two sorts of intimacy: physical and psychological. As we get to know someone better, so our access to their body and their soul increases. Friends, especially female same-sex friends, are permitted to touch one another more often and in a greater variety of parts of the body than are casual acquaintances (Jourard 1964) and the nature of a relationship can be seen in terms of a map of accessibility: the hands are available for almost anyone to touch, but knees, for instance, are parts reserved only for persons that we know quite well.

The same applies to psychological intimacy, as we shall see in more detail later in this chapter. The more you know someone, the more you are granted access to their inner feelings, fears, and concerns. The more that individuals "self-disclose" (that is report their inner feelings), the more they are offering friendship and intimacy, as long as they do this appropriately and match it to their partner's disclosures.

7 *Interpersonal perception.* Individuals have views of themselves ("Myself as I am"), of other individuals ("X as I see her or him"), and of such abstract entities as their ideal self ("Myself as I would like to be"). We can also hold views of "Myself as my friend sees me." One line of research (e.g. White 1985) argues that understanding between people is greater to the extent that there is a correspondence between A's "Myself as I am" and B's "A as I see her or him", for instance. In other words, if my perception of you matches your perception of yourself, the better the relationship will be. My understanding of you is also increased, of course, if we are actually similar. In exploring and developing this notion by means of interpersonal perception instruments, White (1985) showed that wives are consistently better at understanding their husbands, even when the two of them are not similar, than their husbands are at understanding their wives. Wives tend, on the other hand, to see themselves as more in agreement with the

husband's attitudes despite the degree to which they are really similar. They seem, therefore, to take a more positive view of their relationship than husbands do. Wives are also more accurate at predicting their husband's response to an item than husbands are at predicting their wife's response, a finding that is possibly due to the (undesirable, but real) power difference in the traditional marriage: it is generally more useful for a person low in power to be able to predict the actions of another who has greater power than the other way round, which perhaps helps to explain why students spend so much time trying to understand what teachers like to see written in answers to their favourite questions!

8 *Commitment*. As individuals grow closer together, so their commitment to one another increases. The degree of commitment can be used by researchers as a barometer or measure of the strength of their relationship. What "commitment" essentially means is some sort of determination to continue and respect a relationship in the face of adversities or temptations (Johnson 1982). Examples are exclusivity, if the relationship is a sexual one, and a tendency to put the other person's interests on an equal or greater footing than one's own. Those who give up their own life for a friend show great commitment though most of us are prepared to demonstrate commitment to another merely by staying in the relationship – either because we want to or because we have to, a distinction that Johnson (1982) identifies by the terms "personal commitment" versus "social commitment."

Hinde's (1981) scheme thus provides us with a set of dimensions on which to assess the nature – and by implication the development – of a relationship. We could measure casual, mid-range, and close relationships on the above dimensions and find key ways in which they differ systematically. We might ask whether close friendships show particular patterns of interactions or communication as compared to the other kinds of relationships, or we could track relationships through their lives and note the changes that occur (see Dickens and Perlman 1981; Duck 1983; Duck and Gilmour 1981b; and the further reading listed at the end of this chapter for work on relationships across the life-cycle). When relationship development is charted, we do in fact find that much of friendship development is banal and repetitive activity rather than being a dramatic and intense increase in intimacies (Duck and Miell 1986).

Kelley *et al.* (1983) have developed a somewhat similar set of eight categories for defining the interdependence necessary for relationships:

1 kinds of events;
2 patterns of interaction;
3 strength of interconnections;
4 frequency of interconnections;
5 diversity of interconnections;
6 interchain facilitation versus interference (that is the extent to which the thoughts or actions of P facilitate or interfere with the thoughts or actions of O);
7 symmetry or asymmetry of interconnection (cf. Hinde's thoughts on reciprocity/complementarity);
8 duration of interaction and relationship.

The model behind this category list stresses that interdependence of the two individuals in a relationship is an essential element to relationships and relationship development. In the terms adopted by Kelley *et al.* an individual's relationship to another person is defined and predicted by the relationship of thought and action processes in the two individuals concerned. In this approach the feeling felt by one person toward another is a consequence of each person's thought about the other and the interrelationship of their thought processes about each other and their lives together. According to this scheme, the most important element of a relationship is the feeling generated by the thought generated by the interdependence of the two persons. Thus relationships can be categorized or distinguished in terms of the eight properties in this list. Kelley *et al.* (1983: 37) give the example that "the relationships of close friends and of husbands and wives are characterized by high strength, frequency, and diversity; symmetry; and high mutual facilitation." (Note that this formulation makes the usual, but to my mind incorrect, assumption that because two people are married they must be close psychologically. The same assumption has persisted in the literature on social support, which has often used a person's marital status as an automatic indicator of the existence of a close relationship without checking whether the married people themselves actually see the relationship as rewarding and close. Yet many married couples see their marital relationship as not close or rewarding at all). By contrast, more distant collegial or task-based relationships would be characterized by Kelley *et al.* (1983) as having low or medium strength, symmetry, and high mutual interference. The scheme is also proposed, as is Hinde's, to offer a way of conceptualizing development of relationships through stages of intimacy, based on changes in the above features.

Another theorist, P. H. Wright (1984; 1985), argues that the dimensions of friendship are several. For instance, a degree of voluntary interdependence is important, but so are the degrees to which each person can serve the other's needs, provide stimulation and support the other's ego (utility value, stimulation value, and ego support value respectively). Furthermore, a "difficult to maintain" factor influences friendship: even if two people love each other, it is hard to sustain a relationship if one lives in the USA and the other in the UK. Additionally the valuation of the person qua person can be important (in other words, the extent to which we like that person as a unique individual). In short, there are for Wright many different dimensions that are simultaneously important in friendship as it is experienced and as it is defined in the scientific studies. Some of these reflect our general needs as human beings and only some of them reflect our evaluation of – and reaction to – the other person as an individual, whether affectively or cognitively.

Human concerns that we take with us into relationships

We can see even from this brief selection of theoretical approaches, together with those listed in Chapter 2, that there are several ways of addressing the issue of identifying the nature of relationships; one can focus on the behavior of people in relationships, on the two people's cognitions of each other, or on various attitudes and behavioral dimensions that can be extracted by measurement scales and careful analysis of the experience of relating to others. Since theorists take different positions and focus on different themes, it is too early to make a proper critical assessment of the different themes and their roles in the whole enterprise (but see Duck *et al.* 1988). However, it can be seen that we can explore a whole range of different elements in studying the development of friendship. It is not simply a question of measuring growth in partners' feelings for each other. One highly relevant aspect of friendships is that we enter them with all the human needs and anxieties outlined in Chapter 1. These are more likely to influence our behavior and our styles in interactions than some of the pioneering research (and even present-day research) has been able to register. If our human concerns make us worry about other people's perceptions of ourselves, it is likely that, for example, we shall try to gather information about their reactions and try to help them to reach the conclusions that we would like them to reach!

Duck and Miell (1986), in charting the development of friendships, found that a major element that directed actions was extreme uncertainty about the other person's feelings towards oneself and the likely stability of those feelings. Friends adopt the view that the existence and future of the relationship depend much more than 50 per cent on the feelings and choices of their partner. We seem to be aware of the risks of the other person "going off us" and we are constantly concerned about it. The intriguing aspect of this is that both parties simultaneously do this and believe that the other person has control! Naturally these beliefs direct their behavior and probably go a long way to explaining why there is such concern over gathering information about the other person: we need to check and "round out" our beliefs about the likely endurance of their feelings towards us and the extent of their commitment to our relationship.

Baxter and Wilmot (1986), in a similar study, found that developing relationships are more carefully monitored by females than by males. Partners also appear to be suspicious of too much similarity or stability. If we expect relationship development to be turbulent, we become anxious and concerned when it is not!

Whatever it is that develops when relationships come into being, another feature that people seem to be aware of is that there are turning-points in their relationships as they develop and these are significant points of psychological upheaval, adjustment, or turmoil (even if the result is ultimately the growth of the relationship, stimulated by the resolution of turmoil: Baxter and Bullis 1986; Braiker and Kelley 1979; Surra *et al.* 1988). We recognize that relationships – particularly courtships but also friendships – have certain stages where emphases will change and be modified (Baxter and Bullis 1986; Hays 1988; Cate and Lloyd 1988). As Duck (1977b) claimed on intuitive grounds, a linear model of relationship growth is not supportable: we rise from plateau to plateau rather than up a continuously rising gradient of intimacy. Relationships develop in steps, not in slopes.

Getting acquainted

Self-presentation

The previous section abstracts the initial conditions for development of relationships – the expectations and concerns that we bring with us – and could be accused of representing it as something disembodied from our real-life actions in relating, just as most research has done (Duck 1986). We all know that when we meet new people we take active steps to try to impress them, if we like them, partly as a result of the concerns in the above section. We also know that we think about relationships and people as we take baths or cook meals, so do the above theories really assume that relationships occur only when the two people are face to face? Recent research has begun to look at some important ways in which we approach the whole issue of developing relationships in an active, thoughtful way.

When we look at the ways in which people help themselves to develop relationships we can identify several interesting features. First, but only recently recognized in this context, is the fact that we must first choose whether or not to "regard" someone as a possible partner. Rodin (1982) argued that the criteria for liking and disliking are not complementary or opposite ends of a continuum but in fact are completely distinct from one another. She argues that the first decision we make in viewing someone else is whether to eliminate them from our concerns. If we decide to "disregard" them, we do not process information from them even if that information would be relevant to forming a relationship; if, however, we choose to regard them, we consider their attributes and their potential as relational partners. Thus, Rodin argues, we do not necessarily process all the information that others provide for us. If we have first decided that they do not count, their behavior and their personality characteristics will be disregarded: however likable these attributes may be, we simply will not notice or act on them. If we decide that we are interested, however, then the other's attributes will be processed to see how likable they are, or to what extent they would be good partners.

Another focus for investigation deals with the ways in which we present ourselves to others, and show what we have to offer other people as relational partners. This can be done in a number of ways, but the most skillfully investigated means are effected by affinity-seeking strategies. Bell and Daly (1984) show how we can take an active role in making ourselves likable to others: we do not simply sit back and let them be impressed or not – we set out to influence their judgements and to make them adopt our perspective or form a positive impression of us. We try to make them come to like us. Bell and Daly conducted surveys of students' beliefs about strategies used to do this. They show that we do this in a number of ways that "locate" us as normal members of society (for example by being polite or by giving out information about the ordinary lives that we lead) and by more active means that show we are interested in the other person's life (such as asking questions that include them in the conversation). We also take steps to indicate our own trustworthiness as partners (whether by talking about other friendships we have or by testifying to our own ability to respect confidences). We also show trust for others by revealing personal information ("I do not tell everyone this, but . . ."). By such means, Bell and Daly show, we indicate to other people not only our attractiveness (we hope) but also our attractedness and our availability for, or interest in, a relationship with that person. By signaling such things we probably also signal the appropriateness of their "regarding" us, in Rodin's term, so that they will process us as stimuli in a much more careful and attentive way than might otherwise be the case.

What do we need to look for?

While the previous section points to the fact that we sometimes (maybe often) try to influence others to like us, most often we are constrained by social conventions and cannot either ask someone if they like us or tell someone directly that we like them. It is inappropriate to turn to a stranger and say "I think you are great" unless we are prepared to risk their saying "So why should I care what you think?" Even feeling secure enough to say "I love you" can take time. Because it is threatening to put our social selves so much in jeopardy, we also avoid risking a strongly negative answer to the question "Do you like me?" by refraining from asking it straightforwardly. Kurth (1970) has argued from a sociological background that this accounts for human indirectness in both indicating liking and assessing it. Typically we use a lot of non-verbal signals such as smiling, gaze, and eye contact to indicate liking indirectly without expressing it verbally, or else we ask a lot of questions and respond encouragingly to the answers, set up "chance" meetings, and so

forth. Not only the initiation but also the development of relationships progresses by indirect means: invitations to become more
involved with someone are usually cautious and ambiguous (the
phrase "Would you like to come up to my place for coffee?" being an
example where "coffee" is sometimes a shorthand for "a more
intense relationship").

The process of signaling interest in or willingness to become
involved with someone else thus entails some quite subtle and skilled
efforts (Duck 1983). One under-researched means of doing this is by
flirting and recently Sabini and Silver (1982) and Montgomery
(1986) have begun scientific work on this topic. Sabini and Silver
have argued that the purpose of flirtation is to encourage the other
person to acknowledge sexual interest, but to do so in such a way
that the issue is not forced, to play for time, and to enjoy the whole
game for its own sake. Flirtation is therefore ambiguous; it has to be,
because once it ceases to be ambiguous it is no longer flirtation and
becomes a blunt or direct sexual proposition. Montgomery's work is
complementary to this position, and also makes some useful distinctions. In a series of studies she found that flirting serves a variety of
purposes, the main one being to express friendship (although women
see this function as more significant than do men, who, rather
predictably, see flirtation as having more sexual overtones than do
women). Flirting is also used to test the target's responses to the
implied interest in a relationship: by flirting, a person indicates
interest in a relationship through indirect means (that is by not
actually asking a direct question) and, by responding positively and
equally indirectly in a flirtatious manner, the target indicates willingness to accept the invitation. However, since the two sexes view
flirtation differently, it is possible for crucial misunderstandings to
arise and to cause serious difficulties when one partner intends a
sexual message, has the message accepted because the target sees it as
merely friendly, and then mistakenly acts as if a sexual acceptance
has been received, rather than the friendly response that was intended. Montgomery's (1986) work is important, therefore, not only
because she takes a new approach to a neglected topic but also
because of these intriguing new findings. (A possibility worth further
investigation and pointed out to me by Paul Wright is that there may
also be something of a self-affirmation attempt in flirtation: that is
there may be an attempt to test out one's own attractiveness to
others without any real intention of "following through." A long-
married person may flirt with an acquaintance as a means of seeing

whether the old magic is still there; a positive reaction from the acquaintance would be ego-boosting even if nothing further developed).

At the point where a full relationship might begin to be established, then, our main objectives are: (1) to appear in an attractive light to the other person; (2) to look for signs of approval and interest from the other person; (3) to signal our interest in that person; (4) to create opportunities for meetings where the relationship could be pursued. Only one of these tasks is purely cognitive. At this point, then, our reactions to the other person are quite superficial, and as the relationship proceeds we need more information.

Active, passive, and interactive strategies for information-gathering

Once we have established our interest in a person and their interest in or liking for us, we can begin the information-gathering that has been emphasized in much research, particularly in communication science. We should not assume that this is always done directly or even that it is done in the presence of the partner. We can reflect on our interactions with people, remembering and replaying a conversation and even planning what we hope or intend to do in the future (Duck 1980a). It can be argued that much relationship work takes place in private when we are on our own: it is simply called thinking, but its products can be future action, invitations to dates, letters, diaries, plans, and much else besides, all of which directly influence relationship development.

Berger and Bradac (1982) have postulated a set of techniques and strategies by means of which we gather the sort of information about partners that will reduce our uncertainty about them and build up a better picture of their personality and their suitability as a partner for us. Such strategies can be passive, active, and/or interactive. Passive strategies are those where people gather information by unobtrusively observing the target person. For instance, we may watch the person dealing with other people and thereby acquire information about his or her personal styles. Active strategies do not involve interaction between the person and the target, but the person does take active steps to gather information (for example by asking third parties questions about the target or by actively structuring the environment in such a way that it requires a reaction or response from the target). Interactive strategies involve direct interactions with the target other person, such as conversation. They are not necessarily always a better method of acquiring information about a target because he or she might deceive us or engage in impression management or other strategic action (Berger 1988). Indeed, Douglas (1985) finds that a primary type of information-seeking (87 per cent of all questions asked in acquaintance) is the use of demographic and opinion/preference information at the start of the uncertainty reduction moves. As a matter of fact, the interactional performance of the other person is not much used as a source for initial uncertainty reduction. It would appear that we are aware of the risks that Berger (1988) identifies.

By these strategic means of information-gathering we increase our comprehension of the other person's nature and obtain a better grasp of the ways in which they think and behave, relate and interact, and conduct their lives or exercise their priorities. Each piece of new information contributes something to reducing our uncertainties about them as people and about the likely success of a relationship that we might create with them. However, as Planalp and Honeycutt (1985) point out, this model is optimistic in so far as it assumes that all information will reduce our uncertainty about another person. Increasing amounts of information can actually heighten uncertainty if the new information is contradictory or difficult to fit in with what we already know (e.g. "S/he reads Plato in Greek and attends the opera, but now I find out s/he loves Jerry Lewis films"). The focus of the uncertainty reduction has also to be considered: increasing our certainty about a partner's faults is likely to be destructive, even if decreased uncertainty in this case may be good for us if it saves our getting into an unsuitable relationship. Sometimes, moreover, we might find out that a partner has lied to us, told our secrets to other persons, or two-timed us in the past. This sort of information can, of course, increase our uncertainty about them rather than reduce it. However, it does reduce our uncertainty in other ways, in that it refines our judgements about their (un)suitability as partners, and might make us more certain that we do not want a relationship with them.

Douglas (1987) reminds us that relationship development is two-sided since both people have a choice and take action to learn about each other. The information-gathering strategies of one partner alone cannot sufficiently explain relational action. Necessarily, we trade off efficiency (that is gathering all the information we need and doing so in the shortest possible time) and politeness (which disallows efficient intrusiveness into other people's business or background). Douglas (1987) surveyed student subjects' strategies for coping with this and showed that this conflict is particularly salient to individuals at the very opening moments of a possible relationship, where they are very keen to know about the possibilities of developing a relationship, yet cannot do so directly in a socially acceptable manner. He asked subjects to list the strategies that they might use to solve this problem and found that the general approach entails a surreptitious testing of the other person's affective judgements and a search for unobtrusive clues to their liking of us. For example, one strategy is confronting (e.g. "I put my arm around her: it made her say yes or no"), another is withdrawing (e.g. "I stopped talking for a while to see if she was interested in picking up the conversation"), and another is hazing (e.g. "I told him I lived 16 miles away and needed a ride home. I wanted to see if he was interested enough to go to all that trouble"). It is clear from Douglas's (1987) intriguing and innovative work that such affinity testing early in relationships is a major social task.

Self-disclosure and open communication

One significant aspect to uncertainty reduction focuses on the trustworthiness of our partner – is he or she the sort of person who can be trusted with our secrets? As Kelvin (1977) has observed, a key element in developing relationships is that we make ourselves more vulnerable. We usually tell our new partners increasingly secret or private information about ourselves and we do this as a measure and indication of our liking for them. However, that information – because of its very nature as private, secret, important, and revealing – puts a powerful weapon in his or her hands if he or she should ever want to harm us. Our vulnerability increases to the extent that we reveal ourselves to the other person – indeed, the paradox of relationships is that increased intimacy and consequent security also increase risk and potential threat. A major concern of persons in dissolving relationships is precisely that the secrets revealed during the extended process of developing relationships will be used to harm us or gain revenge for the breaking up of the relationship (Duck 1982b). In dealing with the invasions of privacy that are willingly permitted as relationships develop, we should keep in mind that this two-edged sword placed in the hands of friends can return as a sword of Damocles when we are dealing with the destruction of relationships rather than their creation and development.

We know that as relationships develop there is a change in the non-verbal invasions that are permitted (Jourard 1964). The same is also true of verbal information: a certain amount of intrusiveness or revelation is permitted and encouraged to develop as the relationship grows and this has been called "self-disclosure" (Jourard 1964). As Sprecher (1987) has shown in a survey of close partners, the important effects of self-disclosure come from not only the amount of information that a person discloses to a partner but also the amount that the person feels the partner discloses. If we feel that our partner is open and disclosing with us, our feelings of liking or love for them are increased. The total amount of disclosure given and received is actually an excellent predictor of whether couples remain together over a four-year period (Sprecher 1987).

There is much more tit-for-tat at early stages in self-disclosure, and much directness and predictability in the way in which it occurs between people. Direct questions are much more common in the early stages of relationships and are answered appropriately, matched fairly often by a return question to the questioner about a similar matter. It is acceptable to ask direct probes about facts ("Where do you live?") or opinions and attitudes at this stage, although the areas of questioning are usually restricted to less intimate matters, like politics. At the outset, some of the questions are very limited in scope and could be restricted to such obvious but banal matters as the exchanging of names and details of home town, type of job, and family or marital status (Knapp 1984).

At these early points in a relationship, then, the range of topics is usually fairly neutral and public, with opportunities for great personal revelations reduced and restricted (Knapp 1984). Indeed great revelations at this stage are irritating and may well lead to negative evaluations of the questioner or discloser (for example to an assessment that the person is weird, unstable, or a mere bus-load of problems looking for somewhere to park – E. E. Jones and Gordon 1972). At different stages of acquaintance, however (particularly the early stages) self-disclosure is expected and is prized: there is a "norm of reciprocity" (Gouldner 1960) in self-disclosure that results in partners matching their disclosures measure for measure, although this tends to wear off as the relationship progresses. While a global balance is still expected in long-term relationships, the specific matching of disclosure with disclosure dies away. In many studies the subject's measure of intimacy in a disclosure has been rated by an experimenter and tested against the measure of intimacy in a disclosure returned by the subject's partner. Thus "My secret fears about my sexual inadequacy" would be typically rated as an intimate disclosure, whereas "My favorite music" would be seen as personal information that is not truly intimate (cf. J. D. Davis 1978). It is clear from a number of studies that the intimacy level of a relationship is often advanced by one of the partners' strategically releasing more intimate information than is usual in the relationship and the other partner responding with equally (increased) intimate responses (see Miell 1984 or Miell and Duck 1986 for a summary). By careful testing of the likely response to such disclosures (for example by making a jokey non-disclosing reference to the topic), the partners are able to assess whether it is safe to make the full disclosure, and so perform a secret test of the appropriate intimacy level for that relationship and of the partner's commitment to it.

In sum, there are various expectations about this potentially intimate sort of communication:

1 you self-disclose if you want to be liked and approved;
2 the amount of self-disclosure must not be too much in the circumstances, particularly to start with;
3 self-disclosure should be matched to the intimacy level of the relationship (which could be changing, therefore self-disclosure can be used to escalate or de-escalate relationships);
4 one person reciprocates the other person's disclosures (and likewise can influence the growth or decline of the relationship);
5 self-disclosure changes and expands as the relationship grows.

We should not accept too readily the idea of information having fixed intimacy value. Not all information can be classified so easily and much of the intimacy value of a given statement will depend on the circumstances in which it is made (Miell 1984). It depends not only on where but also to whom the statement is made (Montgomery 1981). As we get to know someone better, so the threat from disclosure reduces and thus the significance of certain disclosures reduces if they are made to that person, even if they retain their privacy and significance in the presence of other people. What we can learn from this finding is that the same piece of information can have different ratings and meanings, depending on the circumstances or the stage reached in relational development. Information that is highly prized in many settings, where open and frank information exchange is valued, can in other circumstances be regarded as highly negative and repulsive. Think about how you might react if a friend burst into tears and told you that he or she is worried about being unbalanced because the color blue has suddenly become very frightening; now how might you react if a total stranger came up and said the same thing?

The changes that take place in self-disclosure are only part of a general pattern of change in communication that takes place as relationships grow. As Duck and Miell (1984: 233–4) claim, development of relationships not only is an increase in certain affective features such as intimacy, but also involves changes in the form of the relationship. For one thing, as relationships develop so power changes and language comes to reflect implicit partner-beliefs about the relationship (Morton *et al.* 1976). A teenager saying "I'm taking the car – is that OK?" has a different relationship to the parent from one who asks "Please can I have the car?" As Morton and Douglas (1981) make clear, subtle changes like this are occurring throughout the development of a relationship and they serve not only to transform the relationship itself but also to signal to each partner that the transformation has occurred.

Furthermore, as part of these transformations of communicative style, partners rapidly develop "personal idioms" (Hopper *et al.* 1981). In other words, they create personally meaningful language that serves to bind them together and simultaneously exclude other people. For instance, if a couple uses the phrase "Time to do a Mr Johnson," it may mean to them "I'm bored with this so let's leave and go home before it gets any worse" – but no one else would know that and the couple can communicate the idea to each other without any risk of anyone else knowing what is happening. Although it looks as if such phrases are simply secret codes they do serve to create a feeling of specialness in the relationship.

Strategies in self-disclosure

Miell (1984) and Miell and Duck (1986) have shown the extent to which we use self-disclosure strategically in relationships. The work used both interview techniques and direct observation of real encounters in a series of studies on this topic. One important finding from the research is that people "float" intimate topics before they disclose about them seriously. For instance someone may make a joking reference to exams to help them gauge the partner's reactions: if they get a sympathetically toned reaction, they will go ahead and make the full disclosure about their very intense anxiety about the exam; if not, they will not pursue the issue. It is also clear that we sometimes self-disclose not for its own sake but with the strategic purpose of inducing self-disclosure by the other person. Thus, because we know that there is a norm of reciprocity, we may make an intimate self-disclosure so that the pressure falls on our partner to make an equally intimate disclosure to us (Miell 1984). Making self-disclosures oneself is also a way of relaxing the other person and can be an effective strategy in counseling or giving informal advice (Duck 1983).

The strategies of self-disclosure are somewhat different for the two sexes. A study by Derlega *et al.* (1985) focused specifically on finding a case where men exceed women in disclosure, in contradiction of the more usual finding that women typically exceed men in levels of self-disclosure. It was found in an experimental study of actual disclosure exchanges that men take the initiative in comparison to women in directing self-disclosure in first encounters and actually exceeded women in self-disclosure with acquaintances in order to control the development of the relationship, at least in opposite sex encounters. These unusually high disclosures were strongly correlated with liking for the partner and with perceptions of the partner's positive feelings towards the self. If a male subject felt that a female partner particularly liked or trusted him, he was more likely to increase self-disclosure. In other words, a man who suspects that a female partner likes him will increase his self-disclosure as a means of signaling trust, liking, and a desire to have the woman self-disclose in return in order to develop the relationship to a more intimate level.

When does avoidance of self-disclosure help a relationship?

Although openness is highly prized in western cultures and we are encouraged to disclose to our partners (indeed we may be rejected by them if we are not willing to self-disclose), there are certain circumstances where it is inappropriate, as we have seen (for example too early, too much, or too negative a reflection on the discloser's past or personality). Furthermore, as Baxter and Wilmot (1985) have shown, there are topics that create tension in relationships and which partners therefore avoid making the subject of self-disclosures. By means of ethnographic interviews the authors solicited accounts of topics that were "off limits" in their current opposite-sex personal relationships. Results indicate that these "taboo topics" can be such things as past, deep intimate attachments that the discloser has had (which carry the implication, therefore, that the discloser has had former deep attachments that did not survive, so this present deep attachment may go the same way). As another example, "the state of our relationship" is a taboo topic which may launch a discussion that shows all too clearly that the partners have discrepant or incompatible views of the nature of the relationship and its likely future, or future ending. For example, one partner may think that the relationship is heading towards marriage, while the other has always regarded it as a casual relationship.

One thing we should not do directly, even at a later stage, is to ask too openly about the partner's commitment. It is taboo to focus too specifically on the current state of the relationship, the reason presumably being that if we ask too clear a question about it we may get too clear an answer – one we did not want or expect. However, as indicated in the earlier discussion of the Duck and Miell (1986) studies in Chapter 1, uncertainty about the state of that relationship is of paramount importance and interest to people in relationships. So how do we solve that pair of conflicting problems? How do we find out the state of the relationship without actually asking? Note that this problem is both similar to and different from the problem tackled earlier by Douglas in his work on affinity testing: in both the need is for an assessment of the relationship's potential, but in Douglas's work on affinity-seeking strategies the issue concerned the opening moves in a relationship. At the later stages discussed here, the question is how individuals establish the state of their long-term and probably serious relationships, although the taboo against direct enquiry is probably as strong here as in the initial stages of relationship formation.

What do people do to solve this dilemma? Baxter and Wilmot (1984) provide the answer: we use "secret tests." In a study with three distinct stages, the authors first conducted ethnographic interviews in which respondents discussed a current or recent opposite-sex relationship. Next a cluster analysis and Multi-Dimensional Scaling were performed on the resulting prototypical strategies. The third stage was a reanalysis of the interviews, examining gender and relational type in terms of the information-gathering strategies. The results are intriguing and informative about our human ways! If we want to know how much commitment our partner feels towards us, we find out indirectly by confronting him or her with tests, the results of which indicate the level of commitment in subtle ways. For example we may dwell on the attractiveness of other potential partners and we secretly gauge the extent of the jealous reaction that we get from our partner as we tell the tale. If our partner becomes very jealous, we know that he or she likes us a lot. Another method stems from the implied results of a public presentation of the relationship: for instance one might suggest "Why don't you come down and meet my parents for the weekend?" To accept such an invitation is to be willing to have the relationship acknowledged by significant outsiders and thus indicates willingness to accept commitment to the relationship. These familiar techniques are some of the ways in which we get answers to our questions without asking them directly. Even "no answer," evasion, and "playing for time" tell us something about the partner's commitment (or lack of commitment) to the relationship. However, it is also possible that the misunderstanding of the meaning or intention of the partner's response can lead us into a false sense of security or could produce an avoidance of direct discussion and communication which might ultimately be to the detriment of the relationship. Even if the secret tests are conducted, it does not, of course, follow that direct communications are thereby rendered redundant.

Beyond cognition

Liking, trust, intimacy, and so on, are clearly important in the conduct of relationships, but are by no means the end of the story. For one thing, the individual's personality needs and his or her ability to interact skillfully both have an influence on sociability and social experience (see Duck 1983 and 1984 for examples of research supporting the argument that friendship is dependent on such needs and skills and that it may be possible for researchers to suggest ways of improving friendship in distressed individuals – and even in the normal population). It has nevertheless been very easy and meretriciously attractive to researchers to view relationships as simple creations of the feelings of two people for each other, while other researchers have been seduced into the reduction of relationship conduct to sets of rules and skills (see Argyle and Henderson 1985b for a review). However, significant contributors to the success of the relationship – and indeed to the development of any sort of relationship at all – are the partners' aptitudes for conducting the negotiated action that is necessary for them to work together as a couple and to live together as partners. While feelings and skills may be helpful stepping stones on the road towards satisfying relationships, even feelings lead to action and the intertwining of lives through joint action, shared activities, common leisure time, sexual interaction, and a variety of other social behaviors that further enmesh the two partners into each other's everyday lives. To represent relationship growth as a purely cognitive or clinically decisive action is unfortunately and unnecessarily limiting. Appreciation of this point is increasing, however, and recent research is moving sharply towards a consideration of the unnoticed, unconscious, routine interconnectedness of the two partners' lives, including the influence of other persons and outsiders also (Duck 1977b; 1986). Chapter 4 therefore examines the place where those influences and occurrences are most significant, the place where a voluntary relationship between two separate lives gradually transforms itself into a highly committed (and, in a sense, involuntary) relationship that transforms these two people into one social unit: courtship.

Summary

This chapter examined the ways in which development occurs in a relationship and it pointed to the research evidence showing that such growth is not automatic, not smooth or linear, not based solely on intimacy or feelings, and not based on cognitions or uncertainty reduction alone. In discussing the cognitive side the point was made that perceivers are not simply passive processors of information but have active purposes in their social intercourse. It dealt with the strategies through which people manage the vulnerabilities of becoming intimate or of increasing trust and it considered self-disclosure as an element in growth of relationships. In outlining the view that a consequence of greater emotional involvement is greater enmeshing of two individuals' lives it provides the basis for Chapter 4 on courtship progress.

Further reading

Derlega, V. J. and Winstead, B. A. (eds) (1986). *Friendship and Social Interaction*. New York: Springer-Verlag. This is a collection of papers on the theoretical and empirical issues surrounding friendship and social relationships. Particularly relevant to the material in Chaper 3 here are the chapters by Milardo; Winstead; and Berg and Clark.

Duck, S. W. (1983). *Friends, for Life*. Brighton: Harvester. This book develops the argument that friendship can be developed as a skilled activity and it considers the ways in which friendships can be enhanced and improved. By contrast with Chapter 3 this book devotes considerable space to the issue of children's friendships and the problems of "faulty" development of social experience.

Duck, S. W. and Gilmour, R. (1981). *Personal Relationships 2: Developing Personal Relationships*. London: Academic Press. This book collects together papers on the development of friendship and courtship through time and across the life-cycle. There are three chapters on the growth of relationship intimacy during acquaintanceship and seven chapters on the changes in relationship during the life-cycle that are particularly pertinent to the material here.

Foot, H. C., Chapman, A. J., and Smith, J. R. (1980). *Friendship and Social Relationships in Children*. Chichester: Wiley. This is a collection of papers dealing with children's and adolescents' friendships. Several chapters consider the issue of whether these relationships develop in the same ways as those of adults.

Perlman, D. and Duck, S. W. (eds) (1987). *Intimate Relationships: Development, Dynamics, and Deterioration*. Beverly Hills, CA: Sage. This book is a collection of papers, two of which deal with the development of intimate relationships in a general way and two more of which deal specifically with courtship growth. You might want to read the chapters by Kelley and Rolker-Dolinsky; Buunk and Bringle; Baucom; and Acitelli and Duck in the light of the discussion in the present chapter.

DEVELOPING A STEADY AND EXCLUSIVE PARTNERSHIP: COURTSHIP

Most people marry at some point in their lives and most people therefore experience that form of relationship which, at least in western cultures, is preliminary to marriage, namely courtship. According to a survey I once ran in class, the average 22-year-old Iowan student has been involved in 3.45 such serious relationships since the age of 16 and the experience of developing them (and breaking them off) is quite familiar in that age group. While the earliest research on this topic examined the types of people who married (for example by recording their race, religion, economic class, and so on) more recent work has explored the processes of courtship itself and has been more concerned with courtship progress and courtship styles than with the broad social categories that are associated with stable or unstable marriages.

Accordingly this chapter explores the research on courtship taking a broadly historical approach in order to indicate the conceptual developments that have recently built on the pioneering work. Nevertheless there are some methodological points to note at the start. Typically people seek a marriage partner most actively between the ages of about 16 and 26, the median ages for first marriage in the USA being 24.6 years for men and 22.8 years for women (National Center for Health Statistics Monthly Vital Statistics report for June 1987). This pattern represents a development towards marginally later average marriage, begun in the 1970s and continuing into the 1980s (Rogers and Thornton 1985; Norton and Moorman 1987), and thought by some to be due to couples' greater willingness to delay marriage in order to allow each partner to develop a career (Blumstein and Schwartz 1983). Most research therefore looks at young couples. Young people are not the only ones who marry, especially now that the increasing divorce rate releases older individuals to enter second marriages. The results of studies reported here, however, are invariably derived from subjects below the age of 30 and one can assume that the results would have been different if the subjects had been older. For instance, second marriages usually follow a briefer courtship than do first marriages (M. D. Newcomb and Bentler 1981) and older couples meet one another in different ways from younger ones (for example older couples are more likely to advertise, use dating services, or meet through singles-support organizations: Woll 1986). Such differences and potential differences are exciting topics for future study but because of space limitations and the relative scarcity of such research at present, I shall concentrate on the work on younger couples. For similar reasons, I shall confine my remarks to romances between opposite-sex partners; readers may have their own ideas about the degree to which what I have to say here applies to gay and lesbian relationships.

Courting disaster: some early research approaches

Because courtship is a halfway-house between casual dating on the one hand and marriage on the other, a fairly natural assumption is that some force operates to drive it forward or give it momentum. Readers should note the value judgements that are associated with this topic and this style of research into it. Those value-laden styles of thinking – which still pervade our common-sense view – assume that people who stay in relationships are "successes" and people who leave them or are left by partners have "failed." As we shall see in Chapter 5, these value-laden judgements of success and failure are not only unfair but also often problematic for people in disturbed relationships. A corollary of this value-laden approach is that people celebrate lengthy relationships (for example by ceremonial marking of silver wedding anniversaries), since, on this model of marriage, they are the most "successful" ones. On the other hand, over-lengthy courtships are viewed with skepticism and a culture has its own views of the appropriate length of time between first meeting and marriage – not too short, not too long – although we shall see in this chapter that couples act differently with respect to this convention.

One obvious candidate as the engine for courtship progress and relationship "success" is love for one's partner: as love grows, this "theory" would claim, so the relationship deepens and broadens;

eventually the two partners realize that they were "made for each other" and decide to get married or move into a live-in-lover relationship of some kind. Although this force has probably been implicit in many approaches to courtship progress, love has only recently become a focus for research and theory in any dramatic way (e.g. K. E. Davis and Latty-Mann 1987; Hazan and Shaver 1987; Hendrick *et al.* 1984; Hendrick and Hendrick 1988; Kelley *et al.* 1983; Marston *et al.* 1987; Sternberg 1987; Sternberg and Grajek 1984), although occasional essays were produced throughout the 1970s (e.g. Berscheid and Walster 1974; J. A. Lee 1973; Z. Rubin 1970; Swensen 1972; Tesser and Paulhus 1976). It is impossible, in the present book, to do justice to the variety of approaches presently available, so I will have to select a number of points to make about a subset of the work. Some theories see love as a relatively unique emotion and they typologize its manifestations into different varieties that are broadly distinct from one another. Thus J. A. Lee (1973) and Hendrick and Hendrick (1988) identify and work with six basic types of love ranging from self-sacrificing love of the kind shown by Christ and Gandhi to the passionate/romantic/erotic love shown by almost everyone else. Such theories essentially propose typologies based on profiles of the different sorts of the same basic emotion, without explaining its origins. By subtle contrast, some theories also create typologies, but do so from a set of other variables, like commitment, passion, and intimacy, each of which is itself a different thing from love, but which can be mixed together with the others in order to create forms of love (Sternberg 1987). Thus while Lee's approach describes the fact that different forms of love exist and can even be mixed together to form subtly shaded blends, Sternberg's theory proposes that the forms of love derive from independent psychological structures and processes that are brought together to create different clusters of love processes. In other words, Lee's theory creates a typology of love by looking at the ways in which love can be manifested, whereas Sternberg's approach indicates that each form of love results not from other forms of love but from entirely separate emotional/cognitive structures.

Hazan and Shaver (1987) have recently proposed that adult styles of loving may be similar to those noted by workers on childhood attachment. Ainsworth *et al.* (1978), working with children, proposed that there are three styles of attachment to caregivers and Hazan and Shaver have used these as their guide. Secure attachment and loving are characterized by confidence and security in intimacy, while avoidant attachment and the avoidant style of loving are characterized by lack of acceptance of others, avoidance of closeness, and discomfort with intimacy. The final style, anxious/ambivalent attachment and the anxious/ambivalent style of loving, is characterized by dependency and a certain amount of insecurity coupled with feelings of lack of appreciation. Using this system, Hazan and Shaver have shown that this approach helps to identify several aspects of love and social experience. All such approaches ultimately assume that love – or ability to love in particular ways – is the product of mental operations in the context of emotional experience, while other work does not necessarily explain where love comes from, but sees it as manifested in, and facilitated by, certain behaviors and circumstances. In the work on courtship that preceded the recent work on the nature and description of love, theories about its nature were often undeveloped or implicit, and they broadly assumed that we know what love is and that it promotes satisfaction and development in courtship. Adopting such an approach either explicitly or implicitly, much early research was devoted to the discovery of static or global factors that predicted love and hence courtship progress or marital success. Among a relatively unimaginative and predictable list of such factors are the matching of partners' characteristics; the partners' demographic origin or background; and their personality characteristics, specifically the influence of partner similarities or individual differences that existed prior to the courtship.

Unsurprisingly, then, given its historical context, work on courtship tended to begin with such basic assumptions. It was assumed that courtship proceeds on the basis of two suitable or matched individuals falling in love with each other – however that occurs – and progressing gradually and thoughtfully through courtship and engagement to marriage. It was a slow, careful business that occurred between appropriately paired adults roughly 22 years of age or over (Kerckhoff 1974). Essentially it was still held to be true, as Goffman (1952: 159) stated, that

> A proposal of marriage in our society tends to be a way in which a man sums up his social attributes and suggests to a woman that hers are not so much better as to preclude a merger or partnership in these matters

and that such attributes and attribute-matching were about all there is to it – a "theory" currently espoused by dating agencies.

Research therefore focused on the issue of the specific stimuli or characteristics that best predicted the progress of courtship or were the best correlates of ultimate stability and satisfaction in marriage. The question addressed by such research was: what kinds of people get into the most stable and happy relationships? The answers tended to refer to religion, economic background, race, age, intelligence, and so on (Kerckhoff 1974). It was repeatedly found, for instance, that couples who married young were likely to experience instability in marriage and had a higher risk of divorce, and recent research indicates that, by 1985, 32.4 per cent of women who first married before the age of 20 have divorced (Norton and Moorman 1987). There is also a relationship between incompleteness of a woman's education and the likelihood of her divorce, since women whose education stops short of a degree or diploma are more likely to divorce than are those who expect to obtain a degree or diploma (Norton and Moorman 1987); however, when highly educated women do divorce, they are much less likely than are other groups to remarry, possibly because their education has enabled them to achieve a career position that facilitates greater economic independence. Low socioeconomic status also predicts instability and unhappiness in marriage (although it predicts unhappiness almost everywhere else in a person's life, too). Couples who have experienced many different sexual partnerships before marriage are likely to end up in unstable marriages (Athanasiou and Sarkin 1974) and it has recently been shown in a longitudinal study that cohabitation before marriage is associated with a much higher rate of divorce than is found in those who did not cohabit before marriage (M. D. Newcomb 1986). In this latter study, over 600 subjects from a variety of backgrounds were surveyed from 1976 onwards and it was found that 22 per cent of those who cohabited before marriage were divorced by 1985, compared with only 9 per cent of those who had not cohabited, a significant difference. When data from men and women are analyzed separately, it is found that men who cohabited did not have significantly higher divorce rate than non-cohabiting men, whereas women who cohabited were significantly more likely to divorce than women who did not cohabit. Thus it may be that those who have experimental attitudes to relationships do not establish exclusive partnerships in as determined a manner as do those who have more traditional views, and that this is true of women to a greater degree than it is of men.

In tandem with studies about partners' demographic characteristics – which soon broadened out to encompass their past experiences and habits – researchers looked at other global personal characteristics (e.g. personality factors) as predictors of original choice and also success in the eventual relationship (Duck 1977a). This research indicated that psychologically distressed people, neurotics, highly ambitious individuals, and people with rigid defensive styles were likely to be "unsuccessful' in marriage, whether that meant a higher likelihood of divorce or merely higher levels of conflict (Murstein and Glaudin 1968).

How courtship grows: some basic views

In so far as researchers studied conflict in courtship it was regarded as a problem, pure and simple, and the researcher's job was to find ways of reducing it (e.g. Haley 1964). Couples who fight and argue must be having a hard time (it was assumed), are doing something wrongly or unsatisfactorily, getting on each other's nerves, and generally making their lives miserable. Therefore conflict must be reduced and techniques have to be developed for dealing with it and minimizing its effects on the couple and their marriage (Gottman *et al.* 1976). Since conflict was regarded as an indication of instability in a relationship, its frequency was often used as a barometer of the relationship's stability or progress (Haley 1964).

In so far as researchers looked at intimacy at all, it was assumed to underlie successful relationships and the intimate feelings of men and women were assumed to be not only comparable but also identical as far as scientific scrutiny was concerned (e.g. Levinger and Breedlove 1966). Only recently have new approaches to intimacy and distance begun to uncover sex differences (and similarities) in intimacy (Helgeson *et al.* 1987) and it is now clear that the progress of a courtship is affected by the degree to which the two individuals differ in their conceptualization and operationalization of intimacy. Instead of being a simple independent variable that operates on the dependent variable of courtship growth, intimacy is itself influenced by courtship progress and has complex interconnections with courtship development, courtship outcomes and subsequent marital "success or failure" (Reis and Shaver 1988). As M. D. Newcomb (1986) has suggested, personality factors may influence perceptions of relationship quality (such as feelings of intimacy) that could themselves influence the actual stability and happiness of the marriage. In brief, then, intimacy is a topic requiring investigation, rather than a factor with unambiguous effects, which may have been the assumption in the early research on this topic.

Such research also assumed that one marriage was much like another and therefore was essentially the same institution and the same sort of experience for everyone (remember the review of magazine advice by Kidd 1975 discussed in Chapter 1). Thus there could be "perfect marriages" and the characteristics of good wedlock could be identified and held up for us all to try to copy. There was a traditional view of marriage that assumed that individual beliefs, individual expectancies, and individual means of conducting the relationship were not relevant (Simmel 1908/1950).

According to this view, where members of society are assumed to have uniform conceptions of courtship and marriage, there is a right way to do it and other ways are wrong, inexpert, or misguided (Kidd 1975). Even that view, however, tacitly assumes that satisfaction with a marriage is not based simply on love, since couples will be able to compare themselves to the social ideal and could judge their satisfaction and success partly in terms of fulfillment of that ideal (Simmel 1908/1950). Marriages are compared to social standards just as other relationships are (G. J. McCall 1988) and our choices of action in a relationship such as courtship are frequently influenced by social attitudes or peer pressure. Christopher and Cate (1982), for instance, showed that men in most courting couples claimed that they first chose to have sexual intercourse as a result of peer pressure ("Haven't you guys made it *yet?*") whereas women felt that they had their first intercourse because they wanted to personally and the level of communication in the relationship was good. Even during courtship – based on personal love, as it is supposed to be – couples compare their own behaviors and experiences to the perceived "norms" and "ideals."

Research on courtship – conducted as it is within certain protocols and assumptions – soon progressed beyond assuming that the total course of a courtship could be predicted from partners' personal attributes as individuals, measured only at the start. In 1962 Kerckhoff and Davis set in motion a new train of thought that led to different conceptualizations of courtship. Their argument was that couples proceed through courtship by reference to a series of "filters," that is couples first assessed each other on the basis of some coarse criterion, say value similarity, and if the partners passed that test, they proceeded to the next test, say need complementarity. In this model partners use series or sequences of methods for testing each other's suitability, rather than one single test. The idea here is that progress through courtship depends on different things at different times: the course of courtship can be influenced at a later stage by elements other than those that influence its beginning.

A similar notion was proposed by Murstein (1971; 1976; 1977) in an approach known as S-V-R theory (for stimulus-value-role), where couples are first influenced by each other's stimulus features (looks, for example) but subsequently concern themselves with the match between their values, attitudes, and so on. Finally, the important feature that concerns them is the role behavior that they perform: for instance whether their respective performances of the role of husband and wife complement each other sufficiently to make a satisfactory working unit for the total relationship. As Murstein's work attempts to show, it is important not only that a given husband and a given wife are each clear about the role of "husband" and of "wife" – whatever they happen to believe those roles involve – but that each of them is capable of performing the role as he or she sees it. Furthermore, their views of "husband" and "wife" roles should be complementary ones in themselves. Thus, their behaviors in the role of "husband" and "wife," as they see them, should match well and the number of daily hassles between them should accordingly be reduced. Such an influence is a relatively late arrival in a given courtship, however, and the matching of partners' role concepts will be irrelevant to the success of the early stages of the courtship.

Some assumptions implicit in these approaches

Clearly some of the pioneering explorations of these issues both answered some questions and raised other, more difficult questions for future researchers to explore. Such work helped to uncover the difficulties with the belief that courtship success was determined by the two partners' attributes at the outset of the relationship, and that successful courtship is conflict-free, or, at least, that all conflict is bad and should be reduced if a couple is to have a satisfactory relationship. Obviously (this assumption goes) conflict is merely disruptive and causes problems without solving anything. This view does not, for example, accept that the experience of resolving conflicts plays any role in courtship and it does not distinguish between one sort of conflict and another. However, Braiker and Kelley (1979) and Lloyd and Cate (1985) have recently shown, in different ways, that conflicts can help to stabilize relationships. After all, there are many issues around which conflict can be generated (ranging from "Where do we hang this picture?" to "How often and in what ways is sexual intercourse to occur?" to "Who is to control the relationship?"). As these authors show, there are many components to the establishment of a relationship that require resolution of differences between two people: it is almost inconceivable that two individuals with different backgrounds would start out by doing everything in the same way, putting the knives in the same section of the same drawer, and so on; and a large part of "making a relationship" is precisely this joint construction of a shared experience and routine (cf. Levinger and Breedlove 1966). Thus not all conflict will hinder a relationship: some sorts of conflict promote relational growth by being a major part of the process of relationship creation. So the "obvious" point about conflict is not the whole truth.

Equally "obvious" to this common-sense view is the "fact" that everyone has the same idea of what a perfect marriage or courtship is like and that personal preferences for different styles of relationships are not applicable here, since marriage appears to be a fixed relationship and people achieve it either successfully or unsuccessfully. What matters, it is claimed, is the type of background that you have, your age, and the kind of person you are: these determine your marital success. The characteristics of the two partners – even those characteristics that exist before the partners meet – are what counts. Such views are fostered by extensive literature about romance: not only popular magazines, but also the widespread romance novels available in many outlets (Sterk 1986). The couple's behavior in working out their day is implicitly regarded as irrelevant to the development of a relationship – or at least as secondary to the importance of background, "rightness for one another," love, and intimacy. The behaviors of love and intimacy are alone what counts in this conception – and, on such a model, these are capable of being listed: caring, listening, self-sacrifice, for example.

Finally, despite their apparent conceptual advance over some of the other quite simplistic models, filter theories in general have been widely criticized (e.g. Z. Rubin and Levinger 1974). Essentially the argument against them is that they have not yet proved their case, the definition of specific stages and sequences often being so imprecise that a test of their validity is almost impossible except in a very vague way (e.g. by showing that one set of variables apparently operates after another, without specifying the length of its operation or the time in courtship when it is most influential). At this point it is nevertheless safe to conclude that some sequencing of influences has been shown by several authors but that no precision or specificity as to their exact operation has been achieved (cf. Duck and Spencer 1972; Duck and Craig 1978; Hays 1985; 1988).

More recent research on courtship has tended to adopt a number of dramatically different approaches to the issues of courtship growth and marital stability, as well as testing different assumptions about the whole nature of the enterprise, while at the same time incorporating some of the more useful notions from earlier approaches. Some of the more obviously different assumptions are based on the fundamental idea that there are several parts to a developing courtship and that they are influenced by a variety of factors, rather than one factor of paramount importance. They thus adopt an essential idea of filtering approaches without themselves taking such an approach.

Is courtship any different from any other relationship?

If we look at courtship as a process rather than as a state of relationship or as a type of relationship, we can see that it has many parts and we can consider the research in that light – just as we can examine our own assumptions in the light of that new way of seeing things. First, courting or even long-term dating couples have special feelings for each other but only one part of the relationship involves that set of emotions. Courtship and marriage are probably the only types of voluntary relationships that have an exclusivity about them: part of the whole business of courtship is the cutting off of other sexual relationships and the devotion of oneself to a specific partner. Naturally that fact has several important implications, as we shall see, along with other special features of courtship.

The place of courtship in the life-cycle

Courtship usually takes place at one particular period in the life-cycle. Typically courtship partners are aged between approximately 16 and 26. At each end of this age range social pressures are quite

strong and the partners will be especially likely to be sensitive to a
sense of it being "too early in my life to commit myself just yet" or of
"time running out" as they approach the end of that time window
(Hagestad and Smyer 1982; Reisman 1981). It is not just that one
feels love for a courtship partner, then, but that one is also aware of
the appropriateness of the time to express and execute those feelings.
Courtship takes place in a period which is known to last until a
certain time of life, after which the opportunity for courtship dimin-
ishes, as people see their "marketability" decreasing dramatically
with age. Often this makes partners think very carefully about such
questions as "Is this my last chance?" or "Should I commit myself
just now when other, more suitable partners may come along? I'm
still young yet . . .". It may be too early to get married to someone
you love and have known for a year if you both still happen to be 20,
but you might feel that the time is just right if you are both 25, even if
the loving feelings are of the same strength in both cases. If courtship
were about love and nothing else, these issues would not strike
people so forcefully.

Courtship as an experiment

The importance of this point is accentuated by the special nature of
courtship as a testing relationship en route to a known goal (marriage) which allows partners greater leeway to end the relationship if
it gets into trouble. When a *friendship* gets into trouble, the partners
may just let things lie fallow for a while; by contrast, partners in a
courtship will rarely be content merely to ignore or set aside troubles,
problems, or dissatisfactions with their relationships. Once they
suspect that their relationship is not working they will probably
decide to end it. Marriage is intended to be an exclusive relationship
that lasts for life and the purpose of courtship is to test out a future
marriage. Thus if a courtship seems to be working enjoyably, one
stays in it and if it does not work one leaves in order to have a better
chance of finding one which is more congenial. There are thus fewer
half measures or quiet connivings in courtship than there may be
with friends who can fall out without the need to end the relationship
formally or explicitly.

The realization of interdependence that is often created during this
testing causes other issues to surface. Because people recognize the
track-like nature of courtship they know where it is supposed to be

leading (to marriage) and they know roughly how long it usually takes courtship to get to that goal (so several years would be "too long" and three weeks would be "too short"). It should come as no surprise to learn that partners in courtship very often break up at around fifteen to eighteen months into a courtship (Hill *et al.* 1976): by this time the relationship has developed to the point where it needs to be defined. The partners tend to see themselves as being confronted with a once-for-all choice between marriage on the one hand, and terminating the relationship on the other.

Courtship and others' expectations

Another point about courtship has to do with the organization of the relationship (G. J. McCall 1988). Courtship, being a kind of recognizable relationship with a known social form and known expectancies (namely if it "succeeds", it leads to marriage or to live-in loving), has a certain predictability not only for the partners themselves but also for parents and friends. Once one partner has been introduced to the other partner's parents and friends he or she becomes enmeshed in a social network and its own characteristic set of expectancies.

People in some kinds of relationships are treated by third parties as being in that sort of relationship in a way that leads to recognition and restructuring of expectations: for instance, they are invited out as a couple, not as individuals. Furthermore, such social influences can take the control of the relationship out of the hands of the partners themselves and some actions in a relationship may be deferred (for example the partners may decide not to have sex yet) because people other than the partner may disapprove or be upset. For instance, friends or parents may get angry or may disapprove if the unmarried courting partners enter obviously into a sexual relationship and, for example, want to sleep in the same bedroom when they stay at the parents' home. Equally, couples may be influenced by social networks to expect certain activities in their relationship. As indicated above, Christopher and Cate (1982) showed that couples sometimes approach their first sexual intercourse under the influence of friends' expectations. However, such influences can affect even the existence of the relationship as well as the behavior in it. On the one hand is the claim of a "Romeo and Juliet effect" that may occur in relationships where parents disapprove (Driscoll *et al.* 1972), that is couples may pull closer together in the face of parental opposition to the relationship. Other authors are more qualified and claim that, whatever the immediate response, the ultimate result is that parental opposition (or very strong opposition from friends) is more likely to predict the break-up of the relationship (Parks and Adelman 1983). One thing that is certain is that the approval of other people is important and "noticeable": whether we are eventually swayed by it or not, we cannot ignore it very easily.

The relational context provided by religious background can also be relevant here since, for instance, Catholics may progress more slowly in courtship or may stay in unhappy marriages for longer periods of time because of their religious convictions and the influence of those upon their beliefs about the conduct of relationships. As an extreme case, Catholic couples may remain married because they do not believe in divorce, not because they enjoy the marriage or like their partner (M. D. Newcomb 1986). Equally, couples may get into greater conflicts with one another because of differences in their religious beliefs about the sexual components of courtship and how those aspects should be managed (Newcomb and Bentler 1981).

Organization of the relationship is also done with reference to cultural prescriptions, especially as they apply to preliminary relationships like courtship that have a testing function for some other ultimate form of relationship like marriage. Being in a known type of relationship for which strong social expectations exist, couples can evaluate their progress toward normality and the approved endpoint or style of relationship (Fitzpatrick and Badzinski 1985). That is why people occasionally break off the relationship and give the reason that it does not feel as if it is progressing well (either too slowly – "It wasn't going anywhere" – or too quickly – "It just got too intense too soon"). Part of the process of courtship involves the partners' becoming attached to the socially defined role of "being a couple," as well as coming to love the partner (Cate and Lloyd 1988). It takes a considerable amount of effort and accommodation for couples to work out the difficulties of becoming a couple that shares living space, develops routines for doing chores, accommodates each other's needs for privacy and for intimacy, and deals with the requirements of managing sexual interaction (Altman *et al.* 1981). For all these reasons, the organization of a relationship can be problematic for courting couples.

Other aspects of courtship: (1) sex (and possibly violence)

Courtship is different from friendship because it raises the issue of sexuality. Couples who fall in love may feel sexual needs that have to be dealt with in a way that satisfies each of the partners and outside observers. While promiscuity is tolerated in some societies, most have restrictive rules about sexual interaction and people are not generally free to decide for themselves the limits of their sexual conduct and habits. They are expected to abide by the formal rules of the society and will attract censure from others if they fail to do so. The norms about relationship conduct are not always formalized, however, and are often embodied in "social pressure" from peers or parents, even in the form of gossip that can make someone's position awkward and thereby bring him or her back into line (LaGaipa 1982). A couple's sexual habits are regarded as legitimate topics for gossip and peer pressure, such that couples will experience their own sexual needs not only in the context of the relationship itself but also in the context of the wider society. Conflict may arise from the societal context as much as from within the relationship itself (Duck 1986).

Even prior to courtship, it is evident that a reputation for sexual promiscuity is borne in mind by people indicating their availability for dating. In a study of "the elusive phenomenon" of playing hard to get, R. Wright and Contrada (1986) showed that people who were moderately selective in dating were viewed as more desirable than people who were thought to be either generally non-selective or else overdemanding and highly selective in dating. What seemed to account for the attractiveness of such moderately selective people is the attribution that the person is neither too hard to get through choice nor utterly available through choice: they choose to be selective, but not unreasonably so. Availability, then, is best when it is tempered by reasonable selectiveness.

After dating, and once courtship begins, the availability of someone for a date is obviously less of a deciding factor and it is sexual availability that becomes more significant. During courtship, obviously, the management of sexual behavior is an increasingly significant aspect of the relationship. Christopher and Cate (1985) explored the different pathways to sexual intimacy taken by couples moving from first date through casual dating to considering becoming an exclusive couple to actually becoming one. Couples who pass rapidly through the progression (and who may even have sexual intercourse on their first date) experience not only greater feelings of love for each other but also much higher rates of conflict. For couples who move more slowly up the sexual intimacy scale, the increases in intimacy are also associated with increases in conflict, and it seems quite clear that intimacy and conflict go hand in hand in many ways.

As dating intimacy increases so too does violence between partners, as if the positive and negative elements in the relationship are jointly increased. While some studies (e.g. Cate *et al.* 1982; Laner 1985; Makepeace 1981) show a figure around 20 per cent, Deal and Wampler (1986) report results of a survey showing that 47 per cent of individuals had experience of violence in a dating relationship at some point – the majority of such cases being reciprocal, with both partners being violent at the same time. We should be curious about why the figures disagree, and why disagreements are constantly noted and reported by reviewers (e.g. Cate and Lloyd 1988). Clearly there are some problems about the status of respondents' reports – not everyone wants to admit to doing violence or being the victim of it – but there are also different definitions of it, some of it being "symbolic" (such as threatening to hit or hurt someone, but without any real intention to carry out the threat). Not everyone who threatens violence actually does carry out the threat or even means the threat seriously or literally, as parents of young children often exemplify: the threat itself is often enough to induce obedience. Given such problems, still unresolved in this complex literature, it is interesting that Deal and Wampler's figures for non-reciprocal violence indicate that it was the male partner who was three times as likely to report being the victim, a finding very similar to that reported by Cate *et al.* (1982). There are various ways of interpreting this finding; first, men and women differ in their expectations of being on the receiving end of violence and report only those cases where these expectations are exceeded. Second, men, for some reason, feel more secure about admitting to being on the receiving end of violence. Third, men regard more minor experiences as "violence." Fourth, female assertiveness could be interpreted by a male partner as aggressive or violent, whereas the same behavior in a man is perceived "merely" as an expression of male assertiveness. Fifth, perhaps females do resort to physical violence when frustrated, because they have had fewer opportunities to engage in other, non-violent forms of assertive display.

On a related theme, Marshall and Rose (1987) found that some 74 per cent of couples report having expressed violence at some point while somewhere around 60 per cent had received violence at some point in an adult relationship. Once one restricts the data to eliminate so-called "symbolic violence" (threatening to throw or hit or else throwing or hitting an object rather than a person, for instance), the figures are 52 per cent and 62 per cent respectively – but that then refers to "real violence" and is more in line with Deal and Wampler's study. This implies that such violence is far too common and a question we need to explore in future is whether the experience of violence is especially associated with certain points in a relationship, with particular styles of relationship management, or with certain types of partners.

Other aspects of courtship: (2) marital expectations

A couple experiences not only expectations but also anxieties about marriage in a socially defined manner, and in two separate ways: expectations about getting married and expectations about being married. First, Zimmer (1986) explored premarital couples' fears about marriage and found strong doubts about the possibility of maintaining security and excitement in the same relationship. Couples were also anxious about their ability to fulfill themselves. Obviously such fears might discourage couples from getting married. Second, Sabatelli and Pearce (1986) have shown that married couples have expectations about the "proper" level of outcomes in the marriage and found that couples had very strong expectations about trust for a partner and less strong ones concerning privacy and communication about sexual relations. As we shall see in Chapter 6, such expectations often form a background for the break-up of relationships. Yogev (1987), in a survey of American couples, has shown that such expectations and perceptions also occur in relation to marital satisfaction in dual-career couples – an increasingly large subset of the populations in many western societies. Despite the non-traditional behavior of such couples it was found in Yogev's study that marital satisfaction is related to perceptions that spouses fit sex-role stereotypes. Both husband and wife see the husband as superior on most dimensions such as intelligence, competence, and professional status, even in these essentially non-traditional couples.

What is the role of feelings, then?

Attitudes to love and intimacy

Given all that is going on in the background, it is clear that courtships
are not simply about the development of feelings for one another,
even if that were a simple thing in itself. Indeed, the development of
intimacy turns out to be anything but simple, for it is now known
that there are sex differences in intimacy and in attitudes to love. As
Hendrick *et al.* (1984) have shown in their survey of some 800
students in Florida, men and women have different attitudes to love –
and love itself can be divided into six separate components. Essentially, men are more inclined to "low commitment love" with a
strong sexual element while women (who also show those general
inclinations) have in addition a strong practical side to their love,
seeing the importance of checking out a partner's earning potential,
family background, and loyalty. It remains to be seen exactly how
such differences in love attitudes could affect the course of a
courtship or predict (or account for) the degree of stability of a
subsequent marriage (Duck 1986). However, these attitudes are
likely to influence courtship progress in so far as they may create
fundamental differences in perspectives on relationships.

There is now some clear evidence that men and women differ not
only in their concepts of love but also in their view of intimacy and
distance in relationships. It is often found, for instance, that men
appear to regard intimacy as being embodied in joint activities, while
for women the specific activity that signals intimacy is sharing of
information, feelings, secrets, and insights into oneself (cf. Hendrick
1988). In a recent paper, Helgeson *et al.* (1987) report a questionnaire study of students' experiences of distant and intimate same-sex
and opposite-sex relationships. Their results show that there are
more similarities than differences between the sexes with respect to
the meaning of intimacy but that the differences are detectable not
only in and of themselves but also in same-sex versus opposite-sex
relationships. In same-sex relationships, distance is caused by
annoyance rather than by threat (for example if a partner acts in a
silly way after a few drinks) and there is not a big, explosive break-up
as there often is in opposite-sex relationships.

Organization of the relationship

We might well ask what it is that develops in courtship on the basis of all these expectations, attitudes, and differences in perspective. As some innovative work has recently begun to show, what really happens is that people get themselves sorted out as a functioning couple! As we explore courtships as an interpersonal process (Huston *et al.* 1981), so it becomes clear that a major part of the process of courtship deals with the creation and organization of activities in the relationship. A considerable part of courtship involves the sharing of time together and, of course, couples have to work out the means for achieving this for themselves (Huston *et al.* 1981). Huston *et al.* studied recollections of courtship in fifty couples who were in a first marriage of ten months' duration or less. The couples drew graphs to indicate changes in the likelihood that they would marry as they reviewed the period before they eventually did marry. After completing such a graph the subjects also filled out an activity checklist in respect of activities such as leisure, instrumental activity (such as shopping), and romantic activity. The research showed that courtship breaks down into four major types which vary not only in the speed with which the couple decide to get married but also in

Figure 4.1 Average trajectories to marriage for relationship types

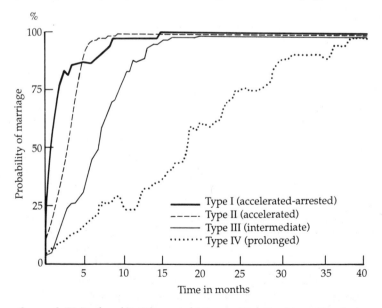

Source: S. W. Duck and R. Gilmour (eds) *Personal Relationships 2: Developing Personal Relationships.* Academic Press: London. Reprinted with permission of Academic Press.

terms of their distribution of activity. "Accelerated-arrested" couples begin with a high level of confidence in the probability of marriage and then slow down their final progression to marital commitment. However, such couples are closely tied to one another emotionally and affectionally. They also spend most of their leisure time together and they typically segregate tasks and chores into those performed by the man and those performed by the woman. "Accelerated" couples start off somewhat more slowly but follow a steady and true track towards eventual marriage. They are typically the closest couples emotionally and also share many instrumental activities. "Intermediate" couples evolve slowly but steadily and do not really experience much turbulence or difficulty until the very end of the whole process. They are rather disaffiliated from one another, having weaker emotional and affectional ties, they spend considerable time alone, do not act particularly affectionately with one another, and are quite separate and segregated in their performance of instrumental tasks. "Prolonged" couples are turbulent and difficult most of the time and progress to eventual marriage is slow. Like the intermediate couples, they are quite unbonded affectionally, do not spend a lot of leisure time together, and typically segregate their roles in performing instrumental tasks.

So what is going on in these different courtships? In the longer ones the distinguishing feature is that the couple spends less time in joint activities and may not express strong feelings for one another consistently. The main point, however, is that there is an important integration between the development of feeling and the creation of joint patterns of activity for the spending of leisure time together.

As a part of the development of courtship, partners develop an approach to their relationship and have to make decisions about it. Surra (1987) has shown that couples in the different courtship types give different reasons for the development or decline of their relationship. Partners in the rapid, smoothly developing courtships not only become more closely interdependent and withdraw from the social network but also tend to feel that the reasons for growth in their own courtship are similar to those generally expected to promote courtship growth. In other words the relationship grows because the person's expectations about relationships match well with his or her perceptions of what actually occurs in the relationship. Things are as they should be, so progress results. By contrast, couples with a slower rate of progress tend to ascribe responsibility for courtship progress to their own behaviors in the dyad; in other words they place responsibility not on expectations but on their own interactions such as conflict or self-disclosure patterns. Discrepancies between the two partners are more often cited as reasons for downturns in the relationship, in contrast to discrepancies between a person's own expectations and actual occurrences.

Summary

The notion that courtship progress depends only on the growth of feelings about a partner is clearly incorrect: many other factors are also involved. It is no use expecting couples to be successful in marriage merely because they are from similar backgrounds or have the same kinds of personalities. Their beliefs about marriage are as important as their behaviors in locking their lives together and sorting out the ways in which their time should be spent in one another's company. As we shall see in the next chapter, these matters also have important ramifications for the maintenance of relationships.

Further reading

Cate, R. M. and Lloyd, S. A. (1988). Courtship. In S. W. Duck *et al.* (eds) *Handbook of Personal Relationships*. Chichester: Wiley. The most up-to-date and comprehensive summary of research on courtship by the authors of some of the most innovative work on this topic.

Huston, T. L., Surra, C. A., Fitzgerald, N. M., and Cate, R. M. (1981). From courtship to marriage: Mate selection as an interpersonal process. In S. W. Duck and R. Gilmour (eds) *Personal Relationships 2: Developing Personal Relationships*. London and New York: Academic Press. Probably the single most important report of the new style of research into courtship, taking and introducing the new ideas that lie behind it.

Jones, W. H. and Perlman, D. (eds) (1987). *Advances in Personal Relationships*, Vol. 1. Greenwich: JAI Press. A bang-up-to-date book of the most recent advances in the field. There are three chapters on love, one on video-dating, and one on emotion that are very relevant to the present chapter.

Perlman, D. and Duck, S. W. (eds) (1987). *Intimate Relationships: Development, Dynamics, and Deterioration*. Beverly Hills, CA: Sage. This collection of papers contains three chapters directly relevant to the issues discussed in this chapter (that is one on romantic relationships, one on the female initiation of relationships, and one on mate selection) and several other chapters with some indirect relevance (e.g. two on intimacy).

5 / MAINTAINING RELATIONSHIPS

Like a good government, good digestion, or a good car, we do not really notice what it is that good relationships do for us when they are running well – unless they are running especially well. Yet relationships, like these other things, seem to need maintenance, or else they fall into disrepair or turn into the kinds of skeleton relationships that are sustained only by the regular but infrequent means of exchanging Christmas cards or birthday greetings. Is that truly a relationship? Do relationships need maintenance or do they endure just because the partners like one another?

In the case of a car, "maintenance" means several things, from keeping it in good running order to smartening up the interior and the bodywork. In the present chapter I consider several things that could be meant by "relationship maintenance." First, one clear sense in which researchers use the term is to refer simply to sustaining the existence of the relationship, and ensuring that, for example, a close friendship does not atrophy or become less close by reason of lack of contact or interaction by the partners. Second, "relationship maintenance" could refer to the regulation of intimacy in that it prevents the relationship from developing a *greater* closeness and thereby stops any escalation. Third, it could mean stabilizing a relationship that has been through a rough patch. I shall reserve detailed discussion of that topic for Chapter 7 (on repairing relationships), although I recognize that repair and maintenance can overlap. As will become clear later in the present chapter, the processes here center on commitment, behavioral coordination, and organization of routines, as well as involving affection and social skills in the management of conflict. However, people do not always maintain relationships simply by intentional means. As has been widely recognized (e.g. Johnson 1982; Levinger 1979), social constraints and family or network pressures can act as barriers to the break-up of relationships and so serve as maintaining forces. We sometimes stay in a relationship to avoid the social consequences of leaving or because of a felt moral pressure rather than because we actively enjoy the relationship and want to stay in it for "interior reasons." "What about the children?" and "What will the neighbors say?" are psychologically powerful questions. Johnson (1982), for instance, distinguished between "personal commitment" (essentially based on a person's liking for the partner or the relationship) and "social commitment" (essentially based on the perception of moral pressures, other people's views, and societal forces). The present chapter is essentially about the ways in which these intertwine but, because it deals with maintenance of relationships that are not necessarily in trouble, will emphasize the personal side of commitment more than the social. Chapter 7, on the other hand, will give more emphasis to the social elements in commitment. Incidentally this topic is a relatively new one in the social psychology of personal relationships, although it has been considered by family scientists. Therefore this chapter covers some recent, ground-breaking research and I shall focus on the conceptual issues that I see this work beginning to address. In five or ten years, I predict, a chapter on this topic will be the backbone of books on relating to others.

When I wrote about this issue in the mid-1980s (e.g. Duck 1983) I followed the then predominant line of thought by proposing that relationship maintenance was a product of relatively mechanical interaction skills. According to that model, relationships are maintained to the extent that partners are skillful in interacting with one another. This view assumes that poor relaters can be trained, through social skills training or advice on communicative competence. I still believe that there is something to be said for that argument but I have now come to realize that it places too much emphasis on special behaviors and ignores the important and overlooked role of the mundane in social life.

As has been repeatedly argued in this book, relationships become integrally involved in the everyday lives of everyday folk. One unfortunate consequence of early laboratory work on relationships was that it stripped them from their everyday contexts and the surrounding paraphernalia of life, such as social networks and daily routines, and focused only on the feelings and affect that people express for one another. In real life, however, much happens incidentally that keeps our relationships together – for instance, the routines of life make it easier for us to meet and coordinate our timetables. If we live close to one another, the difficulties of maintaining the relationship are decreased and we can enjoy one another's company more easily. If two partners have groups of mutual friends, meetings with them also bring the partners together.

These aspects of daily living are so "obvious" that it is easy to underestimate their significance in keeping friendships alive. Nevertheless, we begin to notice their relevance and significance once we come to the point where relationships break down (Morgan 1986). At that point, meetings forced by daily routines or the commonplaces of life and work become especially unpleasant – indeed, people will sometimes leave a good job just to get away from a former friend or partner who has now become estranged. At that point the role of groups of friends also becomes especially important and takes on a different character: you cannot avoid involving them in the breakup. At the very least, friends will have to be told about the split; this can be an unpleasant task in itself, adding to the pain of separation.

Conversely the routines of daily life have an important place in relating to others through their provision of "irrelevant" experiences that nevertheless have some impact on the conduct and maintenance of friendship. Circumstances and daily hassles happen to strain relationships independently of the feelings of the partners for one another. For example, squabbles about daily chores can feed into the conduct of relationships, as can the ordinary hassles of daily life. A bad day full of irritations and frustrations can overflow into the relationship: anger generated by a frustrating day at work can spill over into frayed tempers at home. Such daily events can become the future weapons in a well-sustained battle or even a war that can strain a relationship ("Why do you always bring your work home with you?"). Equally, separation of partners when one of them moves home for occupational reasons can place tremendous strain on a relationship, even though relocation should not always be taken personally. Once again we see that it is not feelings alone that keep a relationship intact; the way we structure our lives and conduct ourselves is also important.

Some of the routines of life keep relationships running as smoothly as a fill-up keeps a car running but, just as refills are not all that a car needs in the way of servicing, so too mere reliance on everyday routines is by itself inadequate to sustain relationships. Although much has been written on the skills of starting relationships (e.g. Argyle 1983; Duck 1983), the real skills – as yet only briefly touched on by research – are those by which people sustain and continue their relationships with one another (Dindia and Baxter 1987; Shea and Pearson 1986). Two friends are not just friends but are also individuals who have their own daily lives to lead, their own personal concerns and projects, their own daily problems to manage. Their every waking thought is *not* about the relationship alone and researchers in the field of personal relationships need to take the lead from family researchers who have examined time budgeting in marriage (Clarke *et al.* 1986). Just how much of the average day *is* spent on relationship tasks, such as planning meetings, preparing surprises, writing letters, making phone calls to friends, and all the other more mundane tasks of gossiping and relational maintenance that take place in the course of helping friends with their daily tasks and personal concerns or projects (Duck 1986)?

Explorations of techniques for maintaining relationships have only recently begun, Ayres's (1983) study probably being the first. Ayres explored relationship maintenance strategies and found it possible to construct a list of tactics that grouped into three categories of strategy: avoidance, balance, and directness. When one of the partners wanted to develop a relationship, the other person who desired only maintenance of the status quo tended to avoid discussion of the relationship's future. If one partner desired the decline of the relationship, the other partner who wanted to maintain the status quo tried to balance things by doing favors, for example. An example of the use of a directness strategy would be simply stating a wish to keep things as they are. Ayres found that relationship types did not affect the choice of strategies but recent work has challenged this finding. Shea and Pearson (1986), for example, surveyed 432 individuals by questionnaire, deriving the sample from groups of utility company employees, government employees, clerical workers, managers, real estate agents, and architects. They found in general that relationship type did not affect the selection of strategies but did find that the partner's intentions for the future of the relationship and the sex-composition of the dyad affected the choice of directness strategy. Women were more likely to employ directness if their male partner desired to escalate a relationship and they did not.

Other recent work confirms that the use of maintenance strategies depends on the type of relationship that we are talking about – whether it is a close friendship or a distant one, for example. Rose and Serafica (1986) asked people what they believed about maintaining their relationships, and found that most people regard their best friendships as self-maintaining and as being more or less entirely based on affection, such that they expect there to be less damage done to them by incidental decreases in contact. Best friendships are expected to last in the absence of substantial maintenance in ways that close (but not best) friendships or marriages clearly do not. Casual friendships, at the bottom of the ladder of intimacy, are believed to require only proximity and frequent interaction between the two partners to sustain them. It seems quite likely that different kinds of relationships require different sorts of maintenance – or even are differentially affected by the need for maintenance in the first place. Some seem to require virtually no maintenance while others need almost constant maintenance. However, it is worth noting that people may well underestimate the extent of any sort of work that they actually enjoy doing – in other words, in the most enjoyable relationships the same amount of maintenance work may seem to involve less effort because it is more enjoyable. By contrast, maintenance work in the least enjoyable relationships may seem more full of effort because it is accompanied by a sense of self-sacrifice or self-discipline. These kinds of feelings could account for the fact that the most intimate (and so most enjoyable) relationships appear to require least effort – or are so perceived by the partners.

Relationships over time: centripetal or centrifugal forces?

Let us start by asking some questions about long-term relationships and how we think of them. Do they just develop to a given level and then stay on a plateau? If it takes all that work to get them to develop, what does it take to keep them there when they have peaked? It is, of course, possible that there are features of relationships that mean that once they reach a given state they stay there. However, we need to consider whether all long-term relationships are the same when it comes to maintenance needs.

One way of phrasing the central question here is "Do relationships fall apart unless they are maintained, or do they stay together unless they are taken apart?" Some theorists (e.g. Levinger 1979) have taken the former view and others (e.g. Altman *et al.* 1981) the latter. In considering the question, it is easy to focus only on the rewards and costs of a partnership, for example the looks, intelligence, and charm of a partner, and the difficulties of leaving, as against the partner's unattractive work habits, selfishness, or boringness, and the attractiveness of alternative relationships (Michaels *et al.* 1986). It is important not to forget, however, that all the research reviewed so far has shown that many of these aspects of partnerships tend to lose their power as time goes by and that the elements that assume greater importance are the mundane routines of everyday life. Thus the presumed reward value of positive cues decays with time and other aspects come to the fore (Berg and Clark 1986).

In the array of constancies that face us in daily relationships, one is the instability of those relationships. We should remember that we are continually making decisions about staying in a relationship: we do not make such decisions once and stick with them forever (Duck and Miell 1986). At any point in the life of a relationship, the partners could decide to get out, although the longer the relationship and the more central it is in their lives, the less likely this is and the harder it is to do so. People weigh up the efforts against the preferences more carefully in longer-term relationships and should experience a greater degree of stress in leaving them.

One approach to satisfaction and dissatisfaction of relational partners has been developed carefully by Rusbult (1987). In a series of studies she has looked at the ways in which couples deal with dissatisfaction and has identified four category labels or symbols for broad sets of interrelated behaviors that characterize reactions to felt dissatisfaction. These four categories are *exit* (getting out of the relationship or thinking and talking about getting out, for instance), *voice* (discussing problems, seeking help with problems, talking things through, for example), *loyalty* (waiting for things to get better, hoping things will all sort themselves out, for instance), and *neglect* (for example, ignoring the partner, treating the partner badly, just letting things fall apart). As can be seen, these fall along two axes: an active–passive axis (exit and voice are active, while loyalty and neglect are passive) and a destructive–constructive axis (exit and neglect are destructive, while voice and loyalty are, in some circumstances anyway, constructive). This model has generated much useful work on the demographic and gender differences in response to dissatisfaction, but it remains for future research to establish how such issues relate to the *process* of falling out and recuperating from disruption (see Chapters 6 and 7 of this book for process models of each).

In developing both a typological and a process model, Lund

(1985) tested a "pull model," consisting of love for partner and rewards of the relationship as an explanation of maintenance of relationships, versus a "barrier model," consisting of investments and commitments that would be lost or given up by leaving the relationship. In a longitudinal study of student relationships beyond graduation, Lund showed that the barrier model provided the better predictions of whether a relationship would be maintained to last beyond graduation. In Lund's terms, commitment refers to expectations and a sense of obligation to the relationship rather than a positive feeling about the partner. We should therefore not overlook the fact that our sense of obligation to a relationship is often a very powerful force that keeps us in it. As we shall see in different ways in the rest of this chapter, and as we have seen in previous chapters, because there is more to a relationship than feelings, there is more to maintaining it than keeping the feelings alive and more to dissolving it than ceasing to like a partner.

Our common-sense conceptualization of relationship maintenance tends to be overly passive. Yet even if individuals really need to be more active, they do not have to do all the maintenance themselves, or all in one go. Some of the structure in and around the relationship helps; the relationship may be of a formal nature like marriage which one cannot leave merely through one's own decision – a court, other people, have to agree to the dissolution – or it may be informal. Also, we like friends and enjoy doing things with them; sustaining our contacts and preserving joint action with them is probably very important.

It is unlikely, then, that the mere longevity of relationships keeps them going, and it is more probable that something else is necessary, something strategic or active that polishes up the relationship. Nevertheless we should recall that as intimacy increases, so also do structural constraints and these could become more important in the long run (Levinger 1979). They constitute strong barriers to exit: it becomes increasingly difficult to leave, so we look into ourselves to see whether we really do want to leave or whether we are prepared to put up with any pain for other reasons ("For the sake of the children"; "It's not really so bad, some relationships are far worse than this" – although cynics and those who have been through the experience personally might note also the powerful force of continued financial stability in such circumstances, the strong pull of familiar property that might otherwise be lost or given up, and the inestimable value of an organized place from which to operate).

Why do people stay in relationships?

Some research on relationships makes it seem that we do little other than think about relationships and that our feelings are reflected in our thoughts or actions (Kelley *et al.* 1983). For example, one prominent and well-established line of thought on relationships is based on a development of exchange theory. There are several exchange theories; in brief, their central claim is that we are influenced by rewards and costs in social behavior, even in attraction, acquaintance, and long-term relationships (LaGaipa 1977).

Thus we might seek to maximize "profit" in a social encounter by trying to reduce our costs (those parts of interaction that are negative for us) and increase our rewards (those parts that are positive for us). This basic idea (Homans 1961) has been developed very elaborately by a number of researchers and theorists so that a person's own positive attributes (intelligence, good looks, for instance) count as "investments" in interactions and people with high investments will expect greater rewards (e.g. compliments) from the other people that they meet (see LaGaipa 1977 for a good review). A person might decide whether or not to maintain and stay in a relationship by assessing the investment/reward–cost ratio involved.

Other developments of these approaches began to take account of other relevant factors and to de-emphasize the simple and crude profit motives of social interactors. For instance, Thibaut and Kelley (1959) introduced two important concepts: CL (comparison level) and CL alt (comparison level for alternatives). A person's comparison level is essentially the average level of rewards/costs that he or she is used to in relationships: it is the base that is expected to be obtained in any future relationship. If my obtained rewards/costs ratio in a present relationship falls below my CL, I shall be dissatisfied with the relationship, whereas if the ratio is above my CL I shall feel satisfied with the relationship. A person's comparison level for alternatives is essentially the expectation that he or she has about the reward/cost ratio that could be obtained in other, alternative relationships. If the reward/cost ratio in any present relationship exceeds my CL alt, I am doing better in it than I could do elsewhere, so I should feel dependent on it and would probably choose to stay in it and

> rather bear those ills we have
> Than fly to others that we know not of
>
> (Shakespeare 1599: *Hamlet*, III. i)

On this line of reasoning, the endurance of a relationship – as far as one individual is concerned – could be due to the qualities of the partner and the relationship, or to the negative or unattractive properties of the perceived alternatives (CL alt), or to the perceived costs of leaving. Research on close relationships has usually taken the view, in line with this tradition of thought, that a key to relationship endurance is to be found in the balance of rewards and costs that the partners experience (Michaels *et al.* 1986). However, a vigorous line of research follows Adams (1965) in portraying social actors as being concerned with the equity of outcomes for themselves and their partners, rather than merely with their own outcomes. According to this model (Walster *et al.* 1978), relationships are maintained by equitable distribution of rewards and costs for both partners.

Other approaches to relationship maintenance, however, emphasize the role of personal choice and individual skill (e.g. Argyle and Henderson 1985a; W. H. Jones *et al.* 1984). For instance, in order to maintain a relationship, a person not only has to choose to keep it going by preferring it to other relationships but also has to have the skill and ability to keep it active by rewarding the other person and enticing him or her to stay involved. One means of doing this is by being a generally rewarding person who shows social skill, warmth, interest in the other person, ability to listen, willingness to give advice or help, and so on (Argyle 1983; Argyle and Henderson 1985b). To the extent that such skills can be personalized or tailored to the needs of the other person, an individual will be personally rewarding to that person and will thereby help to sustain any relationship with him or her.

Another powerful fact in relationship life is that there are duties that have to be performed and rules that have to be followed, although they are rules that make life easier rather than compulsory rules that we are formally penalized for breaking. Argyle and Henderson (1984) showed that the rules for sustaining friendship differ across cultures but that there are some expectations that maintain relationships in any culture. The six most important rules for friendship are: stand up for the other person in his or her absence; share news of successes with him or her; show emotional support; trust and confide in one another; volunteer help in times of need; strive to make him or her happy while in each other's company. Thus a person's ability to sustain a relationship will probably be affected by the extent to which he or she adheres to these rules, although this probably provides no more than the background for relationship maintenance and does not in itself fully account for it. In other words, there may be some factors that promote relationship growth and others, like the rules identified by Argyle and Henderson, that are essential before relationships are possible in the first place, that is, factors whose absence hinders relationships but whose presence does not really promote them very much.

Does maintenance simply retain the status quo?

It is clear that the maintenance of relationships involves more active processes than we might at first suppose. Another point to bear in mind is the fact that the maintenance and development of a relationship are closely tied together in subtle ways: to develop a relationship to a future level of intimacy one first has to be able to sustain it successfully at a lower and prior level of intimacy. Thus successful maintenance will also be affected by the processes concurrently occurring in the development of the relationship. The ability to maintain a relationship might be influenced by, for example, the level of uncertainty about the partner and the corresponding ability to reduce that uncertainty.

As Van Lear and Trujillo (1986) have recently pointed out, decreases in uncertainty about a partner do not occur as consistently as we might expect. These authors had eighty undergraduates take part in a five-week study of acquaintanceship where subjects talked to another volunteer of the same sex once a week for half-an-hour. Subjects were unacquainted with their partners before the study, which was concerned with changes in perceptions during acquaintanceship. In the second week of their study, the more trust someone felt, the more uncertain he or she was; the more this uncertainty, the more he or she felt attracted! Once again, as in the Baxter and Wilmot (1986) study mentioned earlier (Chapter 3), it seems that we prefer a small amount of instability and uncertainty in our relationships and do not expect to find reduced uncertainty as reassuring as theorists have tended to assume. Uncertainty probably serves to maintain relationships by keeping us interested and on our toes to some extent! As Van Lear and Trujillo (1986) note, there is a characteristic exploratory stage to relationship development and while we may need to maintain our interest in the other person, our maintenance of the relationship takes a different tack: we maintain the relationship by disturbing and challenging ourselves through finding out new things about our partner at this stage. Uncertainty reduction maintains the relationship at the earliest stages by reassuring us that we share common ground with the other person, but subsequent relationship maintenance is achieved by novelty and challenge. Given this, it would not be sensible, as work on maintenance of relationships develops, to assume that all maintenance works the same way all the time or takes the same form at all times in a relationship. At different times and stages of relationships it could well be the case that there are different needs for different styles of maintenance, and we should bear that possibility in mind as we review the work.

Since the important influences on a relationship change over time, the work necessary to run the relationship will also change to reflect and bear upon those influences. For this reason we can safely assume that the maintenance of a relationship will require different actions at different points. In support of this idea, Hays (1984) tracked the development of the relationships of eighty-seven students for three months, administering measures of friendship activities, and friendship description (including assessments of intensity and intimacy) every three weeks. He showed that the maintenance of relationships was dependent on partners' abilities to diversify the basis of their relationship and to divide the work of the relationship into leisure time and tasks. Relationships tended to peak in intimacy surprisingly early (after about six weeks) and the features that changed and developed in depth and degree were behavioral patterns, frequency of meetings, diversity of places for meeting, and breadth of activities performed together. In accordance with Hinde's (1981) scheme, outlined in Chapter 3, the relationship began to move from a uniplex form to a multiplex form and progressed from the base provided by the level previously established. Maintenance and development thus intertwine very clearly and significantly. One cannot develop a newer and more intense form of relationship without successfully first maintaining it at a less intense stage.

Dindia and Baxter (1987) offer one of the first empirically supported considerations of the active strategies by which people sustain and maintain their relationships. It is a matter of fact that most of the time spent in typical relationships is not spent in developing or dissolving them but in simply keeping them on an even keel. In contrast to much research, where interest has so far focused on development or dissolution of relationships, our major real-life effort in relationships is probably devoted to relationship maintenance and repair. Dindia and Baxter (1987) examined the strategies for relational maintenance adopted by a sample of fifty couples (one hundred spouses). Their interest centered on the ways in which a person's choice and use of strategies (as well as the range of options at their disposal) influenced marital satisfaction and length of marriage. Some forty-nine strategies were reported, ranging from "talk about the day," "share feelings," and "symbolic contact" (e.g. a ritualistic telephone call at noon to check how things are going) to such strategies as "reminiscing," "compliments," and "gifts." Other strategies such as "seeking outside help," "joint prayer," and "spending time together with friends" also feature in this long list. The couples showed evidence of more extended lists for maintaining the relationship than for repairing it when it had got into trouble. Obviously if the maintenance strategies work, repair strategies are unnecessary, so there is considerable overlap between categories. By and large, however, it seems that the maintenance strategies involve collaborative focus on the daily routines of life while the repair strategies target the relationship or the partner or oneself specifically (e.g. "talk about problem," "give in," "ultimatum"). It was also found that the longer a relationship lasts, the fewer strategies are necessary to maintain it. This may mean either that partners get better at understanding each other and fulfilling one another's needs, or that longer-term relationships begin to become and remain more stable through their own momentum than from attention and "interference" by the individuals in the relationship.

Roles and relationships

I have spent some time examining the ways in which elements other than emotions might affect the maintenance of a relationship. One further feature that could easily be overlooked is found in the roles that the relationship demands and the ability of the partners to perform them in complementary ways. The ability to sustain a relationship requires the proper observance and execution of various relational rules but several of these are less general than those researched by Argyle and Henderson (1984), and they apply to performance of specific roles, such as the role of "husband" or "wife." Individuals differ in their perception of the components of these roles (Murstein 1977) but they nevertheless see them as important aspects of a relationship. Partners will sometimes complain that the other partner, while being a nice person, was an ineffective "husband" or "wife." In such cases the reason for problems in the relationship may be seen as due to poor role performance rather than the nastiness of one person, or as due to a poor match between the role needs of the two partners.

Hagestad and Smyer (1982) have revealed the importance that we attach to our roles in relationships, the difficulty that we sometimes have in relinquishing these roles even when we want to leave a partner, and the powerful hidden force that the labels "husband," "wife," and "friend" exert in reminding a person of his or her particular involvement in a certain sort of relationship. In considering the break-up of a marriage, the partners will occasionally find it hard to unpick themselves from the role of "married couple" (see Chapter 6). The performance of the marital role clearly affects a person's self-image and constitutes a large part of the person's view of his or her place in the community. Other people react to single persons in ways that differ from "proper" reactions to married persons (for example you can ask a single person out for a date but you should not invite a married person). Thus the roles required in the relationship help in some ways to preserve it and maintain the partners as partners.

In part the roles work to sustain relationships because of the ways in which they structure time. Clarke *et al.* (1986) studied the ways in which married partners work out the combination of their variously role-required behaviors in order to structure the efforts of their days and weeks together. They found that, in contrast to the husbands' work, the wives' work was spread throughout the week and weekend, and that much of it continued while the husbands were enjoying private leisure time. Husbands' work did not seem to help to relieve the wife from domestic chores or to extend her time for private leisure, except in so far as the husbands released the wives from childcare duties at weekends. An important means of maintaining the relationship thus seems to be achieved (however undesirably) by wives' accommodating to husbands' routines, rather than vice versa. As a general point, though, it is clear that the role requirements in a relationship necessitate arrangement of, and mutual accommodation to, one another's timetables and preferred activity patterns. Once an arrangement has been worked out (and as we saw in Chapter 4, this can be a stressful, conflicted, and time-consuming accommodation), its existence serves to mesh the partners together, to bring them into one another's lives in interconnected ways, and to give them shared experience about which to communicate, common problems to resolve, and joint memories of their relationship to reminisce about, thereby reinforcing the relationship.

Role of the network

As we have seen, an important aspect of relationships is that they deal with our experience of life, our problems, and our daily concerns. Large amounts of talk with friends are "experience-swapping" exercises or informal advice-giving (Glidewell *et al.* 1982). Human beings verify their experience of the world by talking or gossiping to friends about it, and find ways of improving an attack on daily issues by hearing friends' advice about them (Suls 1977). Gossip often serves a key role as a source of social comparison – comparing ourselves with other people – as Suls (1977) has shown, but it often goes beyond that to a point where both formal and informal advice can be shared, problems aired, solved, faced, and shelved. Such advising can be quite indirect; for example Glidewell *et al.* (1982) found that experienced teachers frequently tell illustrative stories about predicaments they have had and how they solved them, and that they do this in such a way that novice teachers can work out how to solve the problem depicted in the tale without having to humble themselves by asking directly. Gottlieb (1985) indicates that there are many instances of covert social support provided in this way, even though we most often associate our friends with the direct and unambiguous support and help that they provide through performing special tasks like mending a car, as opposed to routine daily choices, reassurances, and concerns ("Do you really think these clothes suit me?", "You've got a microwave, do you think I should get one?", "Do you think I did the right thing?"). We can readily overlook the fact that although we talk to friends at times of particular stress or trouble, their provision of assistance and care is actually rather insubstantial most of the time precisely because it is very regular and pervasive. It takes apparently insignificant forms in the frequent small business of everyday life and is not limited to major help with really crucial life decisions (Duck 1986).

Morgan (1986) points out that the importance of shared knowledge and of discussion of life or common experience is that it is the continuous basis for personal relationships: it is not just something that comes to the fore when one of the friends has a problem. It is happening all the time in unnoticeable ways. Even in our routine daily conversations with friends we unconsciously sustain our experience of the world and thereby maintain our relationship through the commonalities of experience. Why else talk about "the day" and "the people whom we both know"? In other words, the regular and very tiny routine contacts that we have with our friends every day help us to sustain our relationship not only by allowing us to express emotion, intimacy, and feeling, but also because they interweave that person into our daily lives and our human, trivial concerns and make him or her a party to our little projects.

As Milardo *et al.* (1983) have recently shown, there is a certain systematic method to the ways in which we draw ourselves out of old networks and into a new one as we enter a new relationship. In courtship, partners typically pull themselves out of the casual relationships with their network as they develop stronger ties with each other. However, the bonds with close friends are only barely affected by such developments and it seems to be important that we retain contacts with our usual ranks of close confidants when new important relationships begin. On the whole, though, the longer a couple has been a couple, the less they interact with their social network, the smaller the network, and the shorter the interactions they have with those few people on the few occasions when they do meet. Milardo (1982) took the research further and showed that interference and support from the network are both strong. Parents, particularly, try to influence persons as they select marital partners, but the network also serves to sustain and reinforce the relationship by treating the partners as a couple (R. A. Lewis 1973) or by offering aid, support, and – curiously – Christmas presents to tie the partnership or the family together: Cheal (1986) shows that Christmas presents are often given to the couple as a partnership rather than to single individuals within it, thus serving to emphasize the "couplehood" of the pair.

We should recognize the psychological and communicative significance of these network ties in relationships. Not only do they serve to give us all a background against which to understand our experience but also they link us directly to those apparently anonymous abstractions, "society" and "culture." Wellman (1985) provides a careful analysis of the ties in a small social network and the ways in which they serve to connect the members to the broader community, society, and culture. Every community, society, and culture is obviously (although it has not always been treated this way) composed of the interlinkages between the group of people that comprise it and the communications that they have with one another – and at the smallest, but probably most important, level that means the interrelationships that pairs of people have with one another. Societies consist of related communities, which in turn consist of networks, which in turn consist of pairs of individuals. By being members of relationships at all these levels, individuals sustain their membership of society and also maintain their other relationships.

A final subtlety is shown by Larson (personal communication), whose work shows that when married couples are with other people they see the "playful/social" side of one another to a greater extent than they may do in the day-to-day tensions, routines, or boredoms of interaction in the marital home, with tasks to do, sleep to be had, finances to be managed, and decisions to be made. Thus others in a network can help to maintain a relationship by providing opportunities for the two partners to reaffirm their knowledge of the other person's nice and attractive qualities in a variety of settings.

How does all this maintain relationships?

In thinking about relationship maintenance, we could focus on the strategies that people use consciously to sustain them, for it is certain that we do plan our relationships to a considerable extent. However, there are many other instances where the little things of life keep us together over and above any deep and careful calculation that we may perform on the costs and benefits of the relationship. Also we must not overlook the fact that the "glue" in a relationship is often ably assisted by the cohesion supplied by the other networks to which we belong: sometimes our relationships are maintained by our membership of groups that meet regularly without our own direct action, and sometimes other members of the network serve as go-betweens or catalysts for the relationship of a given pair of constituent members (see, for example, Adelman's 1987 work on matchmakers in romantic relationships).

However, despite such cohesive pressures adding their weight to the strong positive affective ties that may already keep a couple together, we sometimes break off relationships, and it is to this interesting and complex topic that we turn in the next chapter.

Summary

Maintenance of relationships is a neglected topic in research and one that deserves fuller attention. It is too naive to assume uncritically that relationships fall apart unless they are held together and equally unsafe to assume that they hold together unless they are pulled apart. The maintenance of relationships is accomplished by a complex combination of individual strategic inputs, mundane routines, social pressures, ritual actions that celebrate the relationship, personal attention to partner's needs, adherence to relational rules, and social skills, amongst other things. Relationships are sustained not merely by people's feelings for one another but also by people's routines, their trivial interconnectedness and presence in one another's spheres of life, by their strategic behavior intended to sustain the relationships and also by the actions and communications of other friends, mutual acquaintances, or colleagues. Maintenance of relationships is tied to their development in subtle but important ways in so far as a relationship has to be satisfactorily maintained at a given level of intimacy before it can be developed to the next level. There is not, then, a simply new and different set of influences that comes into play at "the maintenance stage." Some means for developing relationships are also means for maintaining them. When relationships break down it may be due to faulty maintenance as much as to increased dislike of a partner's personality or to inadequate development at an earlier stage as much as to failure to maintain at the present stage.

Further reading

There is relatively little work on this topic, as has been emphasized in the course of the chapter. Apart from the general works listed below and the research papers specified, readers are advised to follow up specific references given in the text of the chapter, or else to do their own research on the question!

Ayres, J. (1983). Strategies to maintain relationships: Their identification and perceived usage. *Communication Quarterly*, 31, 62–7. One of the very first attempts to investigate maintenance of relationships, this paper generated a list of tactics that factored into three strategy categories: avoidance, balance, and directness. These strategies did not seem to differ across relationship types.

Dindia, K. and Baxter, L. A. (1987). Maintenance and repair strategies in marital relationships. *Journal of Social and Personal Relationships*, 4, 143–58. This study concerns marital relationships specifically and compares strategies for repair with strategies for maintenance (as summarized in this chapter).

Perlman, D. and Duck, S. W. (1987). *Intimate Relationships: Development, Dynamics, and Deterioration*. Beverly Hills, CA: Sage. This book contains some chapters that are relevant even though its concerns are broader than maintenance.

Shea, C. and Pearson, J. C. (1986). The effects of relationship type, partner intent, and gender on the selection of relationship maintenance strategies, *Communication Monographs*, 53, 352–64. This work on maintenance strategies was based on Ayres's original work and refined some of his findings as described in text.

6 / WHEN RELATIONSHIPS COME APART

There is very little pain on earth like the pain of a close long-term personal relationship that is falling apart. The unhappiness and sense of personal rejection and failure are among a whole range of other pains that sear their way into the lives of those in such misfortune. Recent research suggests that the effects of loss of relationships are sometimes extreme enough to induce severe depression and other psychological traumas (O'Connor and Brown 1984), and that they also seem to cause some physical side-effects, ranging from sleeplessness to heart failure (Bloom *et al.* 1978; Lynch 1977). Yet a survey of men in the Detroit area found that only 23 per cent of their close relationships had lasted since the age of 18 (Stueve and Gerson 1977). Less than half (only 45 per cent) of romantic partnerships last longer than two years (Hill *et al.* 1976), and the prediction is that some 40–50 per cent of marriages contracted in the USA in the 1970s will end in divorce – and probably half of those that break up will do so within ten years of the marriage (Johnson 1982). There are enormous literatures on divorce and separation, particularly on their consequences (indeed there is a whole *Journal of Divorce*). In the present book I will perforce deny coverage to much of this material as I cover friendship and romantic break-up, mentioning divorce and separation only occasionally. Readers wanting more detail on these topics should consult the list of further reading at the end of this chapter.

A first thought about relational problems is that we should look for those factors that are antecedents of divorce or marital unhappiness (Duck 1987a discusses the reasons for looking at the problem this way and raises some questions about their usefulness). Early work developed this first thought and did so in the prevailing climate of opinion – where divorce was always "wrong" and something to be prevented, something rooted as much in moral as in interpersonal problems. For this and other reasons, the research at that time paid little attention to the break-up of friendship. Accordingly it focused largely on the demographic factors that were correlated with unhappiness in marriages or which seemed to underlie divorce. The work paints a picture in which breaking parties are either unwilling/unwitting victims of circumstances or victims of moral pathology. Their history is "wrong" or their moral fiber is weak, so they break up. It makes a kind of intuitive sense and a great deal of research has successfully explored the sense that it makes.

For instance, it has been shown that marriages where the partners are younger than usual are more unstable (Bentler and Newcomb 1978) and that marriages between couples from lower socioeconomic groups or lower levels of education are more unstable than other marriages (Mott and Moore 1979; Renne 1970). Couples from different demographic backgrounds, such as different races or religions, are more prone to break up than those contracted between people of similar origins (Cattell and Nesselroade 1967; Jaffe and Kanter 1979). Equally unstable are marriages between persons who have experienced parental divorce as children (Mott and Moore 1979) or who have had a wider variety of sexual experiences and a greater number of sexual partners than average before marriage (Athanasiou and Sarkin 1974). There is also some evidence that the marriages of Blacks are less stable than those of Whites, but it is unclear as to whether this result is robust and it is also unclear as to how such a finding should be interpreted if it were shown to be true (Ball and Robbins 1984). For instance, it could be the case that economic stability is lower for Blacks and that this reflects itself in expressed dissatisfaction with everything about life, including marriage; however, Ball and Robbins (1984) indicate that married Black men are generally less satisfied with life than are unmarried Black men, even when age, health, and socioeconomic status are taken into account.

There are several reasons for wanting to build beyond such work. First, it illuminates some of the elements that are associated with divorce but does not of itself help us to predict which, from a given set of demographically comparable marriages, will break up and which will not (see Duck 1987a for a review). Although many marriages that started when the partners were relatively young will

break up while they are still young, not all of them will do so: some
last until death do them part. Second, given such work we still need
to know about the role played by the behaviors of the couple and to
understand whether conflict is the result of the pre-existing demographic backgrounds that the partners bring with them to their
relationship. Third, we need to ask whether break-up and divorce
should be treated unequivocally as events that we should account
for, predict, and prevent, or rather as extended processes whose
prevention may not always be for the good. Any form of break-up
occurs over time and has an extensive history: few divorces are
instant consequences of single events. We should recognize the
extensive consequences for the future lives of the partners not only as
they negotiate the break-up but also afterwards as they adjust to it.
Fourth, the partners themselves are not the only ones who are
involved in their own break-up. Friends, parents, counselors, judges,
and children may also be involved. In accounting for break-up,
therefore, we need to consider it as a long-term process in the lives of
the partners and their associates. Finally, we should not imagine that
people do not sometimes think about or plan their break-up (or
maybe about how to prevent it).

Recently research has begun, therefore, to look more deeply at the
specific relational characteristics of those relationships that come
apart. What is it about the two partners and their behavior toward
one another that accounts for the trouble that they experience? Do
troubled couples have particular ways of communicating or relating
that are especially ineffective, for instance? Work has also begun to
explore the break-up of friendships and to look at the actions,
strategies, and persuasive techniques that people deliberately adopt
to break up relationships.

Another important new element in the recent work on the dissolution of relationships has been the recognition that it involves a series
of processes that interlock with one another and is not simply an
event characterized by the waning of emotional attachments or a
decrease in positive feelings towards a partner (Duck 1982a). As
Morgan (1986: 412) has observed, the dissolution of relationships
highlights the operation of relational processes, such as interpersonal
judgements, assessments of social exchange, and interactions, that
are present throughout a relationship but go unnoticed in routine
interaction.

Reasons for falling out

If we stop to think about the reasons for falling out of a relationship with friends or lovers, we can see that relationship break-up is likely to have many components, particularly if the relationship is a long-term one that has embraced many parts of the person's emotional, communicative, leisure, and everyday life. Virtually any aspect of life could be the reason given for a break-up. Typically there are more than just a few reasons for break-up, therefore, even though they can be put into a few general, and obvious, categories. A question for research is not only how these classes of causes interrelate with one another but also how they influence the total impact of the break-up on the people involved. Further, we should not regard all break-ups as equivalent in other respects. Some relationships break up early in their lives and some break up later; some break up because of problems endemic in the persons in those relationships and some because of partners' interactional incompatibility; still others are broken up by "catastrophes" like affairs, relocation, or death. Some break-ups are eagerly sought, some are regretted and mourned; some are intended, some are not.

Ineptitude or lack of skills in self-expression

Some people find relationships difficult and puzzling, cannot get into them, cannot sustain them, and experience loneliness or break-up very often (Peplau and Perlman 1982). The usual way of looking at such people is in terms of their lack of social skills (that is to say, in terms of their awkward physical movements or postures, their odd patterns of eye movements, their poor timing of speech, their hesitancy, their inability to ask interesting questions or make comments that involve another person in their conversations, and so on). For instance, lonely persons have been shown by many researchers to be poor conversationalists who do not involve the other person in talk very well (W. H. Jones *et al.* 1985), to be poor at indicating interest in other people because they often avoid eye contact, do not smile enough, and generally signal uninterest (W. H. Jones *et al.* 1984), to be unrewarding in social interaction (Duck 1983), and to display reduced information output in terms of their non-verbal behavior (Argyle 1983). In general, Leary *et al.* (1986) have shown that bores also have these poorly developed styles of behavior and put people off because of their egocentrism and inability to put themselves into another person's shoes. Duck and Condra (in preparation) indicate that the most boring conversational behaviors ("stimulus deficient communications") are those that exclude the hearer or seem to imply that the (boring) speaker does not value the hearer.

The people who are lonely thus seem to have a whole range of social skill deficits that make them generally unattractive for other people to talk to (Peplau and Perlman 1982) – although one remaining interesting issue concerns the extent to which lonely people relate (or try to relate) to different kinds of relational partners from those that others choose as partners. Perhaps their choices of partners are simply unsuitable. Such behaviors and lack of expressiveness not only make lonely or shy people somewhat mysterious and unfathomable to outsiders, but also make them appear to intend to show lack of interest, hostility, and interpersonal withdrawal. We see these people appearing to be uninterested in us, so we become uninterested in them. It is usually clear when you ask them, however, that such people do not intend to convey disaffiliative or unfriendly messages and often seek help to have the problems corrected (W. H. Jones et al. 1984). Nevertheless, the messages that are received by outsiders are invariably messages of distance, unconcern, and lack of interest in social relationships (Burgoon and Koper 1984). These latter authors arranged for shy subjects to interact with strangers and then showed videotapes of that interaction to the shy person's friends and also to strangers. Shy persons were rated as seeming not only distant but actually hostile when their behavior was observed by people who had not met them before. Their friends and associates, however, saw their behavior as being within the normal range for the circumstances, although at the bottom end of that range. Thus shy and lonely people seem to produce behaviors that put off people who do not yet know them, but once they somehow get past that barrier, their acquaintances come to reinterpret the meaning of their behavior and to see it in a more positive and attractive light. Until that occurs, however, their behaviors are offputting. As such, the social skills deficits perpetuate the person's loneliness since he or she does not encourage others to break through something that appears to be a barrier distancing the person from others.

For people imprisoned in the isolating cage of lack of social skill, the initiation of relationships is particularly problematic because no one else perceives them as being interested in relating. In a sense, their relationships usually break down before they get going, but even when they do not, the likelihood is that their potential partners will find them such hard work that the relational soil proves to be unfertile for sustaining living relationships, with the result that their relationships are typically short and unsatisfying (Duck 1983).

In the specific case of marital instability or unhappiness, such researchers as Noller (1985) have identified particular non-verbal and other communicative inadequacies in partners, especially husbands. Clearly these people are less extreme cases than the chronically lonely unmarried individuals described above, yet they show a number of similarities of style and non-verbal communication. Noller and Venardos (1986) show that people who are low in marital adjustment (unhappy and unsatisfied marital partners) are overconfident about the interpretability of non-verbal messages given and received. In other words, they feel sure that they have understood their spouse's intended message when in fact they have not, and they feel sure that they are clearly expressing their feelings to their partner when that spouse cannot understand their emotions on a particular issue. In short, poorly adjusted couples not only are less accurately expressive in their communications with one another, but also are less aware of the lack of accuracy. This is particularly true of the husbands in poorly adjusted marriages and is obviously a self-perpetuating problem (Noller 1985): if you persistently believe that there is no problem to be solved, you will not be successful at solving it!

In addition, as Noller (1985) and Gottman (1979) have shown, distressed couples typically show disrupted patterns of communication over and above such problems. For example, they tend to enter "negativity cycles" with lots of cross-complaining, each person attacking the other for some perceived fault in turn; without ever properly addressing the other person's true concerns about the relationship. They bicker, squabble, and try to score points off each other rather than attempting to resolve issues by conciliatory means or trying to understand the other person's point. Such behavior is certainly not as competent and successful as it could be, and indicates another level at which social skills or interaction management problems can exist.

Rule breaking

One obvious manifestation of the lack of social skills in the people described above is that they (unwittingly) violate some of the rules of relationships. Yet relationships do have rules (perhaps, as indicated earlier, "expectations" is a more appropriate term for them) and we can break off relationships because our partner does not adhere to those expectations or rules (for example if the partner is disloyal or unfaithful or lets us down badly). We expect our partners to be open, to feel and express love or liking for us, and to help us when we need help (Argyle and Henderson 1984). The breaking of such rules, whether intentionally or not, is either tantamount to signaling that the relationship does not matter enough for us to try to follow the rules, or evidence of our general unfitness for close relationships. Violation of other rules (that call for us to stand up for partners in their absence, for instance) signals disloyalty and so violates a major requirement that friends stick together and defend each other's interests as if these were their own.

In their research on rule-keeping in relationships, Argyle and Henderson (1984) found that the breaking of rules was considered a very important cause in the break-up of relationships. However, they also found that the "general rules" of friendship or relationships (as above) were usually adhered to and that invariably the ones that are broken so as to result in relationship breakdown are specifically to do with intimacy and support. Lapsed partners are seen as having failed to trust and confide (or to be trustworthy), or as having let one down when help was needed and when a true friend would have provided it.

Deception

Perhaps the most important rule that should not be broken in personal relationships is the rule that a person be honest, open, and trustworthy (Argyle and Henderson 1985a). To deceive a friend or lover is probably the most certain step along the path of the ultimate breakdown of the relationship (Miller *et al.* 1986). We might expect, therefore, that friends and lovers would, by reason of their greater investment in detecting deception and also their greater familiarity with one another, be better at detecting occasions when their partner was intentionally lying. In a study by Comadena (1982), where intimates and non-intimates observed a person lying in response to a set of standard interview questions, it was found, contrary to expectations, that familiarity did not significantly increase a person's ability to detect lies told by another person, although female intimates were marginally better than male intimates in performing this task.

As Miller *et al.* (1986) point out, however, if we build up trust in a relationship as part of the process of developing it, the suspicion that a friend or lover is lying to us will hardly be the first assumption that we make in interacting with them. Indeed, I would offer a couple of hypotheses about the dynamics of treachery: we might be better at detecting lying in people whom we are getting to know than in those whom we know already, since our skepticism about new acquaintances has not yet been set aside in the course of building up trust. Equally and conversely it could be that we are better at deceiving people that we know well, since we are better acquainted with their thought patterns. For such reasons, then, to discover that a friend or lover is deceiving us is likely to be even more devastating than it usually is to find out that we were being deceived by someone else, especially if the deceit is relevant to the existence or continuance of the relationship (for example it is not just a birthday surprise that has been concealed from us or lied about, but is another relationship that the person has become involved in). Relational partners are, by definition as well as by convention, concerned about relational outcomes and "to be trapped in a lie not only thwarts the immediate objective of the deceit [but] also casts a pall over the relationship itself" (Miller *et al.* 1986: 508). Such an occurrence most often results in a drastic alteration to the relationship itself, unless the deceit had altruistic motives that could reasonably have been intended to preserve the relationship (e.g. deceiving someone about a birthday surprise treat: Hopper and Bell 1984).

Tiredness/boredom and lack of stimulation

We often hear people complain that they are bored in a relationship and need some excitement. A commonly cited reason for starting a new relationship is that the new person has some stimulation value for us and offers novelty and an expansion of our views of the world. We can expect, then, that a reason for breakdown of relationships is that one or both partners feel(s) that the other person no longer provides this type of stimulation. As P. H. Wright (1985) has shown in a series of studies, stimulation value is a major element of friendship and we look to friends and partners for new insights, advice on new ways to approach problems, and challenging suggestions for the progress of our life. If stimulation is a major consideration in the start and maintenance of relationships, we can be fairly certain that lack of stimulation will be a reason for breaking off relationships. Indeed, we find that a frequently cited reason for breaking off a courtship or friendship is that "I became bored" (Lloyd and Cate 1985) or the relationship "wasn't going anywhere" (Duck and Miell 1986). In such cases partners could be expressing several things through those simple phrases (for example that they had expected things to move more quickly and found that that did not happen, or that the partners could not accommodate to each other, or that their partner was actually a boring person). Whatever the subtleties of meaning, the fact is that lack of stimulation in the relationship is seen as a sufficient justification for terminating a relationship or starting up a new one, such as an affair. As we have seen in previous chapters, the expectation that a relationship will change and develop is fundamental to its existence, so that its lack of development, particularly in a courtship, is treated as a good enough reason for it to be ended.

"Other" (relocation or difficulty of maintenance)

Apart from the above factors contributing to the break-up of relationships, there are other elements that can cause dissolution, broadly subsumable under the "difficulty to maintain" dimension of P. H. Wright's (1985) analysis of friendship. Events such as moving to a new job or home, or moving away to attend college, can not only strain a relationship but also reduce the intertwining of lives and lower the amount of contact that is possible on a chance or casual basis. Shaver et al. (1985) noted that one partner's move to college was responsible for the decline of some 46 per cent of pre-college romances and while it may seem "obvious" that such separations would lead to break-up, there is no very straightforward reason why that should be so. If partners' feelings for one another are the true basis for relationships and if feelings are dependent only on the other person's characteristics as a human being, mere separation should have little effect. However it is clear from Shaver et al.'s (1985) work that the opportunity to be in new relationships is too distracting and the pressures to develop relationships that are convenient ones to sustain are simply too great.

Conflict

As noted in Chapter 4, it is a mistake to see "conflict" as being of just one type and as all bad. As Braiker and Kelley (1979) have noted, some kinds of conflict actually promote relational growth and the experience of resolving conflict is unmistakably a positive one for couples. There are several sorts of conflict identified by Lloyd and Cate (1985), however, some of which merely reflect the fact that the couple has not yet faced up to an issue (such as who will handle a certain chore in the relationship or take on a particular responsibility) and they bring their individual viewpoints to it unhoned and unseasoned by thought. Some conflict may be about issues that the partners have previously thought about carefully (attitudinal disagreements, for instance) yet have simply reached different conclusions – so they are on a collision course. Recurrent conflict about such issues not only emphasizes the lack of agreement but also indicates the inability to resolve the matter. As a result, the couple feels badly about the issue and develops doubts about each other as reasonable persons, and this sets in train a whole load of attributional activity that can lead to a steady entrenchment of position, a disaffection with one another, and ultimately a strong falling out (Lloyd and Cate 1985).

Processes of falling out

Given the above as a set of possible reasons for disaffection with a partner or a relationship, what happens when break-up occurs? First, partners have beliefs about causes for the actions of breaking up; they have plans, intentions, hopes, strategies for bringing it about (or avoiding it); they also have explanations for what is occurring, what has occurred, how it has affected them, what they now think of their ex-partner, and so on. Breaking up not only is hard to do, but also involves a lot of separate elements that make up the whole rotten experience.

Rose and Serafica (1986) examined subjects' beliefs not only about maintaining relationships, as we have already seen in Chapter 5, but also about endings of hypothetical relationships as compared with their reports of the endings of actual relationships they had experienced. In the case of hypothetical relationships, subjects expected the relationship to be destabilized by lack of proximity or lack of effort to sustain contact or, in the case of close friendship, by decreases in the quality or quantity of interaction. In the case of real endings, however, subjects were more likely to describe a break-up as due to interference from other relationships and to be an extended – and usually painful – process involving attempts at reconciliation, slow death, and gradual decline of affection, rather than a sudden event. What we cannot, of course, tell from such data is whether that is how things "really" were or whether that is how people choose to remember it. That is an important point to bear in mind below: it may well be that in the case of break-ups people have an even greater tendency to rewrite history than they usually exhibit (Duck and Sants 1983). All of us reformulate our memories about relationships quite dramatically. In the Duck and Miell (1986) studies, comparing contemporary accounts of first meeting with subsequent retrospective accounts, we found that people even changed their stories about where they had first met, and Surra (1987) reports that about 30 per cent of one of her samples of married couples were in disagreement with their own partner by more than one year about when they first had sexual intercourse together! In the case of relationship break-up we can expect that people will be even more motivated to see things in a particular way and to remember the relationship so that it conforms to that viewpoint (Harvey *et al.* 1986), since self-image is very much at stake when relationships break up.

Drawing on the theme of process and sequence in separation, L. Lee (1984) indicates the premarital romantic break-ups typically have five stages. A person first discovers dissatisfaction (D), then exposes it (E), negotiates about it (N), attempts resolution of the problem (R), and then terminates the relationship (T). Lee found that not all relationships break up by passing through all of these stages: some "skip" a stage, but for the most part, these stages are intuitively recognizable and familiar. L. Lee (1984) found, in a survey of 112 such break-ups, that subjects feel that the E and N stages are the most intense, dramatic, and exhausting, as well as the most negative parts of the experience. Subjects who skipped those stages (by just walking out when they felt dissatisfied) reported having felt less intimate with their partner even while the relationship had been going satisfactorily. In cases where the whole passage from D to T is especially extended in time, the subjects reported that they felt more attracted to their former partner and that they experienced the greatest loneliness and fear during the break-up.

In a study with similar objectives, Baxter (1984) explored the strategies employed by people intending to dissolve a relationship and found that there are patterned differences among relationships in the ways in which they break up. They do not all follow the same path but they have their own characteristic patterns that fall into several groups. Eight different trajectories for break-up were identified by Baxter, ranging from "swift implicit mutuality" (or "sudden death," where both partners agree on the termination) to "mutual ambivalence," which revealed a set of multiple disengagements mixed in with attempts at repair and reconciliation, or multiple passes through a termination sequence.

In further work on these issues, Baxter (1986) explored the personal expectations that romantic partners have for their relationship and the ways in which these expectations relate to the break-up of the relationship. Eight primary perceived reasons for the break-up of a relationship bear on these expectancies: (1) partners feel that each of them should expect a certain amount of autonomy; (2) they expect to find a good basis of similarity between the two of them; (3) they expect each other to be supportive of the other's self-esteem and feelings; (4) they expect the other person to be loyal and faithful; (5) they expect the other person to be honest and open; (6) they expect to spend time together; (7) they expect equitable distribution of effort and resources; and (8) they expect there to be some intangible "magical quality" in the relationship. Reasons given to Baxter (1986) for breaking up the relationship usually referred to one of these expectations and pinned responsibility for the breakdown on the violation of that expectancy — usually by the former partner, rather than themselves. Presumably a person's choice of strategy for handling the impending or desired break-up would be influenced by his or her perception of the underlying need for break-up and hence by the individualized account of what was the essential problem in the relationship.

In an indirect way, the work of Hagestad and Smyer (1982) bears on this point, since their consideration of different types of divorce not only echoes Baxter's argument that there are different trajectories for the break-up of relationships, but also indicates that a person's way of handling the divorce reflects his or her perception of the flaws in the relationship. Hagestad and Smyer (1982) identified two main types of divorcing: orderly (where both partners fully and satisfactorily disengage from their former positive feelings about their ex-partner, from their feelings about the marriage and its roles, and from the routines of work and daily life that were built into the

marriage); and disorderly (where one of the above three disengagements was not successfully accomplished by at least one of the
partners). This latter category ranged from cases where one or both
partners sincerely and deeply wished that the divorce had not
happened and would still like to be married to their former spouse, to
cases where the two partners were clear that they no longer loved
each other or could not stand the perpetual conflict in the marriage,
but nevertheless still wanted to be in the marital role – to be "a
husband" or "a wife," to share the dreams and the "walking off into
the sunset together." It is clear from this research that there are many
types of divorces, not just one, and that the process of divorcing
differs across divorces (see Further reading for more detail).

A final point to bear in mind is that people's reflections on their
relationships affect their approach to break-up (see Burnett *et al.*
1987). In an intriguing study by Harvey *et al.* (1986), it was found
that people have particularly vivid "flashbulb" memories of past
loves and that the memories of those loves serve as important
benchmarks in people's constructions of, and approaches to, their
lives, and probably their future relationships. Break-up today sets the
scene for tomorrow's relationships: the degree of eagerness with
which they are sought, the amount of wariness with which they are
approached, and the extent to which the person specifically watches
out for or guards against particular features of the new relationship.
In brief, past break-ups tune up our awareness of what can go wrong
or of which partners do not work for us; we try to learn from that and
avoid the problem next time.

So, as we move on to reflecting about the nature of the extended
process of dissolution of relationships, we should not forget that a
person's way of leaving a relationship can set the scene for beliefs
about future relationships.

A model of dissolution

All of the above considerations help us to move toward a particular
overview of the dissolution of relationships, first outlined in Duck
(1982a; 1982b). This approach sees relationship dissolution as
composed of several different but connected phases, each of which
directs a person's thoughts, actions, and interpersonal communications in characteristic ways. It takes account of the fact that a person
feels uneasy about a relationship before he or she talks to the partner

about it, that there are other persons in a network who contribute to a couple's consideration of break-up, and that a major concern for people is that they leave relationships with some feeling that they have acted correctly or in a manner justified by the circumstances they faced or the people they dealt with (see Figure 6.1).

The intrapsychic phase

We frequently moan about people – our partner, boss, and colleagues included. It seems that that is a regular part of life, not something special and unusual; but it is sometimes a prelude to a break-up. In reviewing the literature on conflict and break-up (Duck 1982a) it became clear to me that there is a phase at which individuals reflect on their relationship and prepare a mental list of its deficiencies, along with those of the partner. At such a phase the exchange balance in a relationship might be assessed (cf. Chapter 5) but that is not really an automatic cause of the break-up of relationships, as some commentators appear to suggest (Huesmann and Levinger 1976). The moaning or complaining phase of breakdown is primarily an internal phase with little outward show, and a person could decide to do nothing on the basis of the arrayed deficiencies. This could be because of a wish to try to put things right, or because of a preference to talk it through with the partner (or maybe to wait for a suitable alternative relationship), or because of inertia, lack of will power, or lack of an appropriate opportunity or mechanism. Whichever is true, break-up is not an inexorable consequence of an imbalance in the equity of a relationship.

At the point where the complaints build up to a measure beyond a certain threshold, I suspect that the person would begin to communicate the problem indirectly at first, by means of hints or "needlings" (Harre 1977). There is some evidence (Duck 1982a; 1982b) that disaffected partners first start to communicate their dissatisfaction this way and then begin a "talking to a wall" style of communication that involves them expressing their views about the partner to someone who provides the necessary ear, but who is a third party, either someone neutral and relatively anonymous (such as a bar server or a stranger on the train), or one who does not know the partner well and will not rush off and relay the information to him or her. At this stage of breakdown, the person is really searching for some self-justification as opposed to any real action.

Figure 6.1   A sketch of the main phases of dissolving personal
relationships

BREAKDOWN: Dissatisfaction with relationship
↓

Threshold: I can't stand this any more

↓

INTRA-PSYCHIC PHASE
Personal focus on Partner's behavior
Assess adequacy of Partner's role performance
Depict and evaluate negative aspects of being in the relationship
Consider costs of withdrawal
Assess positive aspects of alternative relationships
Face "express/repress dilemma"

↓

Threshold: I'd be justified in withdrawing

↓

DYADIC PHASE
Face "confrontation/avoidance dilemma"
Confront Partner
Negotiate in "Our Relationship Talks"
Attempt repair and reconciliation?
Assess joint costs of withdrawal or reduced intimacy

↓

Threshold: I mean it

↓

SOCIAL PHASE
Negotiate post-dissolution state with Partner
Initiate gossip/discussion in social network
Create publicly negotiable face-saving/blame-placing stories and
  accounts
Consider and face up to implied social network effects, if any
Call in intervention teams?

↓

Threshold: It's now inevitable

↓

GRAVE DRESSING PHASE
"Getting over" activity
Retrospection; reformulative postmortem attribution
Public distribution of own version of break-up story

Source: S. W. Duck (ed.) (1982). *Personal Relationships 4: Dissolving Personal Relationships.* London and New York: Academic Press. Reproduced by permission of Academic Press.

The dyadic phase

Once a person feels there are strong enough complaints and grounds for taking things up with the partner, something more has to be done. It is not just a question of weighing up the rewards and costs of a relationship, deciding one does not come out ahead, and then "leaving." Leaving sounds easy if you say it fast, but it actually involves real confrontations, real arguments, real pain, real attempts at reconciliation, and real resolution. After the intrapsychic phase, then, comes the interpersonal mess. A partner has to be argued with!

It is unlikely, even if they were initially attracted to each other by their similarities, that two people will take the same view of their relationship (Duck and Sants 1983) and it is particularly likely that, when the relationship is to be carved limb from limb, the two partners will disagree about the attribution of responsibility for the breakdown. Any revelation of the dissatisfactions mulled over in the intrapsychic phase is likely to cause a certain amount of shock and hurt to the injured party. In turn, it is probable that a person with a problem to discuss will also experience pain, in that if the problem is clearly bad enough to cause the termination of the relationship, that process must be begun; while it is acknowledged but resolvable, both partners may feel the distress of knowing that things are not right for one another.

These are some of the reasons, I believe, why research consistently shows oscillation, uncertainty, hesitation, and infirmity of purpose in partners at this point of a break-up (Altman and Taylor 1973; Altman *et al.* 1981; Weiss 1975). People can often be resentful in a relationship and yet be unwilling to finish it. Most of us know that it is possible to be deeply in love with someone whose faults we nevertheless recognize and we all know that it is possible to be unhappy in such a relationship without the love ebbing away. Oscillations and weakening of resolve seem to me to be perfectly human, but none the more enjoyable for that (Duck 1982a). As partners face up to the consequences of deciding between "break it off" and "try to repair it," they will inevitably confront their doubts and anguishes, and will come into conflict with one another – conflict which has to be dealt with in addition to other pains. Even if they decide to renegotiate the form of the relationship, that has its problems and unpleasant traps (L. Lee 1984), and the whole dyadic phase is full of guilt, hostility, resentment, stress, and a negative communicative style (Duck 1982a; 1982b; Noller 1985).

The social phase

After the partners have done some fighting – and probably even
while it is still in progress – there is an important unseen element to
break-up: getting the support of the surrounding network of friends,
relatives, and acquaintances. It is not satisfactory merely to leave a
relationship: it is important to feel justified in leaving. For this reason
both partners consult friends (and relatives) for advice on the
problem and for extra perspectives on the partner and their own
actions (LaGaipa 1982). The network becomes involved in relationships that are breaking up and has views about them as they spoil
(G. J. McCall 1982). It also gives support to the fighting partners,
takes sides, pronounces verdicts on guilt and blame, and helps to seal
the occurrence of the break-up by sanctioning the dissolution (the
most obvious example being a courtroom where a divorce decree is
pronounced).

The notion that this phase is simply a barrier to relationship
dissolution (Levinger 1979) is important but only partly true and
misses the point that there are really two roles that the social network
serves in the context of break-up. Yes, the social network probably
exerts pressure on a couple to stay together – particularly at the start
of a dissolution – and the fear of what parents or neighbors may
think could well act as a barrier to some couples' splitting up (Duck
1982a; 1982b). However, the network also serves a role that facilitates a break-up once the couple seems to be moving toward one.
Networks are distributors of gossip (LaGaipa 1982) and upholders
of social norms (G. J. McCall 1982). They also serve an important
role in recovery from relationship break-up, by supporting individuals when it has occurred (Harvey *et al.* 1986). Obviously, then,
at this point network members do not act as a barrier to break-up,
since they actually help people to achieve it.

The grave dressing phase

Getting over a break-up involves not only leaving the relationship –
and in some cases dividing up the household, the property, and the
children's access time – but also a realignment of feelings about the
relationship, the partner, and the break-up. As LaGaipa (1982) has
shown, it is a necessary part of leaving a relationship that each person
exits with a reputation for relationship reliability still intact. That is

to say, in leaving, a person should not acquire a reputation for untrustworthiness or disloyalty, since that would poison the possibility of future relationships. For this reason, for reasons of self-justification, and for the sake of creating an acceptable perspective on the relationship, partners who split up do a lot of "grave dressing": the relationship is dead and buried so they start to erect a tablet that says important things about its life and death. This tablet takes the form of a good, credible, socially acceptable version of the life of the relationship and the reasons for its death. As Weber (1983) reports, this very often takes the form of a story indicating that the relationship had a fatal flaw right from the start, that the person worked hard to ignore or correct that flaw but, despite commendable efforts, failed: so the relationship had to die. While a primary role of such stories is this sort of face-saving, it is also clear that the grave-dressing phase serves to keep some memories of the relationship alive and to "justify" the original commitment to the ex-partner (Baxter 1987). Such stories are an integral and important part of the psychology of ending relationships and cannot be written off as inconsequential. By helping the person to get over the break-up they are immensely significant in preparing the person for future relationships as well as helping them out of old ones.

In the field of research on marital and family problems, one growing concern is with "postmarital relationships", "remarital relationships," and family reorganization after divorce. Ahrons and Rodgers (1987), for example, argue the case that divorce is becoming a regular feature of married life expectations and that there is "a shift in ideology – from viewing divorce as pathology to viewing divorce as an institution . . . the study of divorce is no longer narrowly defined within a deviance perspective" (Ahrons and Rodgers 1987: 23). Once divorce is seen as a common transition rather than as pathological, researchers can reasonably begin to attend to a much wider range of issues, such as "getting over" as well as prevention, and as much to the processes of entering new relationships as to those to do with leaving the old ones. With this thought in mind, we can move on to Chapter 7 on putting relationships right.

Summary

This chapter has examined the process of the break-up of a relationship and explored it as a multifaceted and extended series of psychological activities rather than as a simple event. It is a process that emphasizes the complex functioning of relationships and the many elements that they require in order to work properly – elements that function quietly and unnoticed until break-up occurs. The chapter identifies these elements as the internal cognitive evaluation of partner, the behavior of relating to partner, the embeddedness of relationships in the social network, and the stories that people create in order to explain their relationship's existence. In the dying and the death of a relationship all of these "sleeping elements" jerk into vigorous life and make the dissolution of relationships the all-consuming psychological experience that it can easily become.

Further reading

Baxter, L. A. (1985). Accomplishing relationship disengagement. In S. W. Duck and D. Perlman (eds) *Understanding Personal Relationships: An Interdisciplinary Approach.* London: Sage. This chapter explores and reports some of Baxter's extensive empirical work on the breaking of relationships and relates it to the strategic work that people do to disengage themselves from relationships.

Cahn, D. (1987). *Letting Go: A Practical Theory of Relationship Disengagement and Re-engagement.* Albany, NY: SUNY Press. An interesting book presenting a theory about the break-up of relationships from a communication perspective.

Duck, S. W. (ed.) (1982). *Personal Relationships 4: Dissolving Personal Relationships.* London and New York: Academic Press. This is the first collection of chapters addressing many different facets of the break-up of relationships, including different styles of divorcing, the role of gossip and social norms, types of commitment, the influence of processes of relationship formation on eventual breakdown, and the role of persuasive strategies in break-up, in addition to a consideration of attribution's role in dissolution.

Duck, S. W. (1987). How to lose friends without influencing anybody. In M. E. Roloff and G. R. Miller (eds) *Explorations in Interpersonal Communication.* Newbury Park: Sage. This chapter considers the role of demographic background in relationship dissolution and contrasts it with an approach based on communication between partners.

Vaughn, D. (1986). *Uncoupling: Turning Points in Intimate Relationships.* New York: Oxford University Press. A useful and interesting, essentially sociological/ethnographic account of the ways in which relationships break down.

Weber, A. L., Harvey, J. H., and Stanley, M. A. (1987). The nature and motivations of accounts for failed relationships. In R. Burnett, P.

McGhee, and D. D. Clarke (eds) *Accounting for Relationships: Explanations, Representation and Knowledge.* London: Methuen. A detailed, thoughtful, and stimulating description and analysis of the styles of accounting for break-up in relationships.

Specifically on divorce and family matters, a very good recent book is Ahrons, C. and Rodgers, R. (1987). *Divorced Families.* New York: Norton.

There are also two good chapters on these issues by R. H. Rodgers (Postmarital reorganization of family relationships: A propositional theory) and by C. R. Ahrons and L. S. Wallisch (The relationship between former spouses) in D. Perlman and S. W. Duck (eds) (1987). *Intimate Relationships: Dynamics, Development, and Deterioration.* Beverly Hills, CA: Sage.

7 / PUTTING RELATIONSHIPS RIGHT

There are many important reasons for doing research on friendship and relationships but one that is implicit in much that has been said so far is that personal relationships – whether friendship or marriage – do not have a natural tendency to be conducted successfully. Yet they can be major sources of our peak life experiences. Researchers therefore often express, but more often merely imply, the hope that the study of friendship and personal relationships will lead to a greater understanding of the ways in which relationships can be repaired, improved, or enhanced wherever they are presently unsatisfactory. Repair can mean one of three things: helping two people make an unsteady relationship work more satisfactorily; helping one person or both people out of a painful relationship that cannot be made to work successfully; or helping to "repair" an individual after the end of a relationship by facilitating their getting over the breakup or the loss of a partner (whether through divorce, separation, bereavement, or some other cause). This chapter deals with all three, although they are not always as clearly distinct as I have represented them to be here. It should also be noted that one goal of research in relationships may be to make people more aware of relationship processes which they themselves can influence (Burnett and Clarke 1988). For instance, by drawing on social psychological principles it may be possible to enhance people's self-conscious attempts to work at the maintenance and improvement of their relationships. Repair does not have to be done by outsiders; in reporting mostly on work that examines intervention from outside the relationship I am reflecting the bias of the current (and rather sparse) social psychological literature.

I am also going to deal with only a limited range of approaches, since a thorough consideration of therapeutic interventions in families and marriage is beyond the scope of this volume (but see Gurman and Kniskern's [1981] *Handbook of Family Therapy*; Garfield and Bergin's [1986] *Handbook of Psychotherapy and Behavior Change*). Therapy for dysfunctional relationships is widely available and offered from a wide range of perspectives, whether broadly psychoanalytic (and so concerned with past events, particularly in early life, as formative influences on present problem behaviors) or broadly existential (and focused on the present or future). As Christensen (1983: 397) notes,

> Some therapists prefer to see the client alone while others want to see all members of the close relationship. Some therapists maintain a passive, interpretative stance, while others are directive and didactic. Therapists differ greatly in the attention they give to cognitive, emotional or behavioral aspects of the problem.

There are also therapies based on individual analysis and those based on family systems, while some treat the problem in couples therapy. The present chapter focuses mostly (but not exclusively) on such naturally available repairs as may exist from a supportive family or helpful friends or be available to distressed individuals from their own bank of personal resources, but I shall occasionally refer to this large literature on formal therapy.

My approach therefore has a number of personal biases that should be acknowledged. While there are many programs designed to enhance relationships (e.g. Mace 1985; Margolin 1983) and while several programs of premarital counseling and remarital enrichment exist (Ridley and Nelson 1984; Farrell and Markman 1986, respectively), it seems unlikely that any such single program will address all the relevant issues. Just as relationship development, maintenance, and breakdown are complicated processes, as we have seen, so too is the repair of relationships (see Duck 1984a for a review). My assumption is that it will be more successful the more it takes account either of the processes through which the relationship comes to need repair, or of the theory of relationship development that underlies any attempt to enhance the relationship (Duck 1984b). Repair strategies also need to take account of the normal human concerns in which the repair will be embedded, since these are not simply discarded just because a person focuses on repairing a relationship.

Some background for the enhancement or repair of relationships

We have seen in Chapters 2–5 that the creation and maintenance of a relationship are processes with many directly and indirectly influential components. For instance, partners have to be competent communicators of interest, sociable in their interactions with associates, and able to intertwine the parts of their daily activities that, although apparently unrelated to friendship and relationships, nevertheless serve to sustain and enhance the interconnectedness of lives and relationships. We learned also that although relationships are based on feelings of attraction, liking, and love for one another, there are sequences of other behaviors and other unrelated feelings and concerns that are essential to the creation of the working entity that makes up a relationship.

If all of these elements are necessary we can expect Murphy's Law (anything which can go wrong will go wrong) to apply to any of them, such that a relationship could become problematic and need repair in respect of any of them. Partners may not be good at showing their liking for one another (Noller 1985), for example, but they may also be poor at coordinating their activities in the relationship, or may be insufficiently attentive to the leisure time that creates opportunities for strong affect to be developed and sustained (Clarke *et al.* 1986). The comfort of happy times spent in one another's company may be essential to one individual's beliefs in the continuance of the partners' affect for each other: Burnett (1986) showed that "contact" – amount, occasion, frequency, or absence – was mentioned more than any other relationship attribute as a significant element. Clearly partners may doubt each other's love not because it fails to be expressed verbally, but because they fail to see each other putting the relationship first, or because they feel that the other person does not *do* the actions of loving by making time to be together (cf. Kelly *et al.* 1985). If those are the feelings or perspectives that render the relationship unsatisfactory, some readjustment of them would, by itself, help the people to repair their relationship by their own efforts.

Accordingly our consideration of the repair of relationships must have built into it some heed of our theoretical knowledge of how relationships develop and our beliefs about the matters that are important to partners as they develop a relationship. Since relationships break down by stages and phases, as we saw in Chapter 6, it is likely that repair of relationships can also be seen in a stage-like way (Duck 1984a) and that is the way I shall treat it here, echoing the analysis of breakdown provided in the previous chapter.

Relevant here are not only the underlying human concerns, nor even simply the development of relationships, but also the complexity of the nature of breakdown in relationships. Since not all breakdowns of relationships are the same – and indeed many separable kinds of patterns were identified in Chapter 6 – it is unlikely that one simple method of repairing relationships will be equally and totally effective in every case. If a car breaks down with a clutch problem, it is obviously no use fixing the carburetor. Just as clinical psychologists spend a considerable amount of time in identifying the main areas that concern a client in the adjustment to a perceived problem, so too should those trying to repair a relationship first attempt to find out what has gone wrong with that specific relationship and what stage in breakdown it has reached. We should expect it to be reasonable and productive to assume that different repair strategies would have best effect on different kinds of problems.

We have seen in Chapter 6 that the breakdown of a relationship involves many facets not only of affect, but also of behavior and cognition. We have also learned that there are points in the process when one's feelings about one's partner are of secondary significance to the pressures that one feels from the network or one's desire to have one's own version of the break-up dominate the accounts that circulate about the termination. In repairing a relationship, then, it is clear that there will be separate but interlocking components, and that dealing with networks or arranging for network support may be as important and as necessary as other actions that need to be performed.

For all of the above reasons, repair of relationships will be complex and proccssual. Much previous work on repair or enhancement of relationships has tended to be conducted as if simple solutions will work across a variety of populations and/or circumstances (see Duck 1984b for a review). Figure 7.1 represents the different strategies for repairing relationships as they may be mapped on to the model for breakdown of relationships given in Figure 6.1 in Chapter 6. It provides a schematic representation of the argument elaborated below about the different stages of breakdown and how they may be addressed.

Given what we know about the extended processes of development and breakdown of relationships, repair is likely to be complex. It can usefully be viewed as an extended process with components

Figure 7.1 A sketch of the main concerns at different phases of dissolution

Dissolution States and Thresholds	Person's Concerns	Repair focus
1. Breakdown: Dissatisfaction with relationship	Relationship process; emotional and/or physical satisfaction in relationship	Concerns over one's value as a partner; Relational process
Threshold: I can't stand this any more		
2. Intrapsychic phase: Dissatisfaction with partner	Partner's "faults and inadequacies"; alternative forms of relationship; relationships with alternative partners	Person's view of Partner
Threshold: I'd be justified in withdrawing		
3. Dyadic Phase: Confrontation with partner	Reformulation of relationship; expression of conflict; clearing the air	Beliefs about optimal form of future relationship
Threshold: I mean it		
4. Social Phase: Publication of relationship distress	Gaining support and assistance from others; having own view of the problem ratified; obtaining intervention to rectify matters or end the relationship	*Either:* Hold partners together (Phase 1) *Or:* Save face
Threshold: It's now inevitable		
5. Grave Dressing Phase: Getting over it all and tidying up	Self-justification; marketing of one's own version of the breakup and its causes	Help in getting over; social support for person

Source: S. W. Duck (ed.) (1984). *Personal Relationships 5: Repairing Personal Relationships.* London and New York: Academic Press. Reproduced by permission of Academic Press.

that vary in their effectiveness at different points in time. We need to start by looking at the ways in which problems arise and considering whether "special" methods are needed to correct them or whether merely increasing or focusing on "normal" activity, such as "being nice," will do the job for us.

The embeddedness of breakdown and repair in people's lives

In Chapter 1 I indicated the general human concerns that individuals have in entering relationships. Relationships are among the most important features of our lives, yet we are uncertain about our own personal importance to specific other people (Duck and Miell 1986). It seems to me that it is important to regard any attempts at relationship repair as being significantly directed by these human backgrounds. We do not stop having human concerns and interests just because we happen to focus our minds predominantly on the one issue of relationship repair. Our usual psychological and communicative processes do not cease; nor do our normal ranges of reaction become altered by our intention to put right some problems in the life of a relationship.

Relationship repair as a project

Just as we may have other plans and projects that influence or even direct our thought and action during the day, so the project of repairing a relationship can soak up a lot of cognitive energy and time. This is not an incidental consequence of relational repair but should be seen as an important component of restructuring the relationship (Burnett and Clarke 1988; Duck 1986). A plan to repair a relationship will clearly bring certain thoughts, representational schemas, and behaviors to the fore in a person's approach to life. For example a person with such a plan may choose to adopt reconciliatory strategies in dealing with the partner (Dindia and Baxter 1987) and may therefore consciously select unprovocative styles of behavior (Duck 1986). Clearly though, one way to repair a relationship is to make it more enjoyable for the partner, by focusing on his or her needs and discouraging cycles of negative interaction. Such changes and bringing of the relationship to consciousness are likely to affect general attitudes and styles.

For example if everyone is usually uncertain about relationships (see Chapter 1), uncertainty about a repaired relationship is likely to be even greater and more fundamental. I suspect that it will increase relational vigilance and make a person more suspicious or careful in a general way. Ehrlich and Lipsey (1969) have shown that such vigilance has detrimental effects on a relationship because it focuses attention too intensely on cues that may be ascribed more significance than they can bear. For instance, every statement made by the partner has meaning wrung out of it, and non-verbal activities are also sieved and surveyed for signs of mischief, trickery, and betrayal (Miller et al. 1986). Such vigilance also adversely affects the trust that is central to relationship maintenance.

An alternative view, however, is that a certain amount of attentiveness to, or knowledge of, relationship processes will benefit couples in problematic relationships (Burnett 1987). Many commentators argue that communication about relationships is a good thing and that it fosters a correct level of awareness and a helpful enhancement of relationships. I agree that this is possible but the line between awareness and self-consciousness can be very fine and couples are often helped by the presence of a skilled outsider who can guide the awareness of the relationship. By that means a person can foster the need for inclusion without inadvertently and unintentionally spoiling the relationship in which inclusion is desired.

A related point concerning satisfaction of the need for inclusion is that to express that need too clearly or too forcefully is to invite rejection. One can need to be included but must not be seen to have that need too obviously, as lonely people often make the mistake of doing: they seem too desperate (cf. W. H. Jones et al. 1985). In repairing a relationship both partners are in effect expressing their need for inclusion quite explicitly and are also breaking one of the implicit rules of relationships discussed earlier (in Chapter 3): "Don't talk about the state of the relationship directly." Such a breaking of two important rules of relating itself becomes a problem that has to be overcome before successful repair can be accomplished.

The fact that relationships are embedded in such contexts is something that should not be overlooked any more than should some other related contextual and background factors. For instance, through research on the ordinary development of relationships we have learned of the considerable ambiguity of the cues that indicate progress and the development of the relationship, and the consequent misunderstandings that can arise (see Chapters 3 and 4). In the repair of relationships the problem is rather different, in that couples focus so (perhaps too) directly on the development or enhancement of their relationship. That is an odd situation, since the topic is usually stressful, and indeed too much metacommunication ("talk about talk" or discussion of what you hear someone else saying) is highly disruptive to a relationship (see Montgomery 1988 for a review). In the context of their usual real-life expectations, then, by focusing on the mechanics of their relationship a couple can bring about an unfamiliar and disruptive process that, in the rather intense context of relationship repair, could be counterproductive.

Individual backgrounds

Another general life-style issue discussed earlier was the impact of an individual's communication style: if a relationship is problematic because of the ineptitude or lack of skill – or just the simple personal problem – of one of the partners, it is not the relationship that needs to be fixed but that individual. Communication style is known to be disrupted in distressed couples (Duck 1986) and apart from the fact that husbands' individual styles are often peculiar in distressed marriages since they are more negative or inexpressive than are those of wives (Noller 1985; Noller and Venardos 1986), the interaction patterns in distressed families are characteristically odd, too, with strong patterns of monologue-silence-monologue instead of real dialogue (Ferreira and Winter 1974). Thus the relationship itself is not always the problem; rather the individuals in it could be problematic and in need of "repair" on an individual basis.

Memory for social events is also relevant to the repair of relationships since the partners' memories for relational events will clearly structure their approach to repair, their orientation to one another, and their desire for success in the repair. If memories for the relationship are positive (Harvey *et al.* 1986), motivation for repair will obviously be higher than where memories are spoiled (G. J. McCall 1982). However, in most relationships where there has been serious conflict, both positive and negative memories are likely to remain side by side. Also, external factors such as those discussed in Chapter 1 create climates of feeling against which personal experiences are assayed. Thus the fact that it is now widely known that about one in every two western marriages will end in divorce

probably affects a couple's willingness to consider divorce as a
solution to their relational problems (Johnson 1982).

These considerations, then, provide a human and societal context
against which to examine the phases of repair in relationships, by
which I mean to argue that different styles of repair tactic are going to
work better at some points in a breakdown than at others. So we
shall first consider personal causes for breakdown – where individualized repair strategies are most effective – and then go on to
consider various dyadic and social strategies that follow in the
sequence.

Individuals' problems in relating

Social skills for the shy and lonely

Forty-one per cent of the US population claims to be shy and 24 per
cent claims to be lonely (Duck 1986). These are clearly people who
find relationships difficult, aversive, or unenjoyable. As Leary (1983)
has argued, the whole issue of social/relational anxiety is complicated, but in essence it seems that shy and lonely people have
developed images of themselves that make them utterly unconfident
about entering relationships. In the case of some shy and some lonely
people, as we saw previously, they have actually developed styles of
communicating and relating which are unhelpful for other people
and tend to give off messages that are interpreted as showing that the
shy person is hostile (Burgoon and Koper 1984) or that the lonely
person is distant and uninterested in other people (W. H. Jones *et al.*
1985). In the case of lonely people, they may be not merely distant
but actually incompetent in conversation (W. H. Jones *et al.* 1984).
Therefore, the usual advice to "go out and meet more people" is
particularly inappropriate as a starting-point: it is very likely to
increase rather than decrease their experience of rejection unless
their problems at conducting relationships satisfactorily are first
addressed and diminished (Duck 1983).

In all these cases, programs exist to retrain the necessary cognitive
attitudes (Young 1982) or social skills – both at the "macro" level of
conversational strategy (W. H. Jones *et al.* 1984) and at the "micro"
level of non-verbal behavior (Argyle 1983). The repair of relating
skills in these cases is aimed at making the person more expressive
and rewarding to other people, while also giving him or her the

experience of feeling better in social situations. That feeling can feed back to their self-concept and help them to feel more positively disposed towards interaction with other people – more affiliative and inclined to seek affinity towards others.

Problems in developing or keeping relationships

Once such a problem is corrected by therapeutic means or by individual actions, the difficulties in entering a relationship are reduced but the problems of developing relationships are not immediately removed. Some individuals are perfectly comfortable while interacting socially with others but find it hard to develop relationships or to keep them once they have begun. For instance, a large number of people have chronically low self-esteem that renders them uncomfortable in relationships with others (Adler 1929/1959) and they therefore shy away from increasing the intimacy of any relationship (Acitelli and Duck 1987). Low self-disclosers have been implicated in this problem since they fear disclosures that might present themselves in a negative light and, so they think, would put the other person off (M. H. Davis and Franzoi 1986). This lack of self-disclosure itself leads to the very lack of intimacy that would be necessary to reassure such people that they are acceptable to others even with any faults that they may have, and so a vicious circle of withdrawal and distance is established. As M. H. Davis and Franzoi (1986) indicate, such private self-consciousness and fear of exposing one's inner thinking lead to low self-disclosure which itself leads to loneliness and a sense of rejection, which keeps the self-esteem low. Thus those who have problems in developing relationships should be encouraged to be attentive to their self-disclosure patterns (Duck 1983), to invite others to self-disclose to them, to establish an atmosphere in which they and the other person feel able to self-disclose comfortably and to react to their own and others' self-disclosures in a supportive and accepting way. This would involve the absence of expressed judgement about the material revealed, coupled with a willingness to self-disclose one's own experiences on similar counts, whatever the topic. These techniques will bring about more encouraging experiences of social interaction and will prevent the effects of such individualized problems that can lead to constant experiences of undeveloped relationships.

Further evidence of the same sort of problem comes from research

reported by Mehrabian and Ksionzky (1974), who show that neurotics tend to become more insecure and anxious the more intimate
and (for most people) "comfortable" the relationship becomes. A
frequent consequence of this is that neurotics are keen to break off
relationships before the insecurities are actualized: that is to say, they
will break off the relationship in order to prevent the partner from
doing it first! While such behavior is understandable from some
points of view, it naturally deprives the person of the chance to
experience good relationships. It is also insufficiently informed by
knowledge that almost everyone feels insecure in developing relationships and it personalizes the feeling as if the (neurotic) person is
the only one who had doubts about others' feelings for them.
However, recognition of the fact that we all feel doubtful about
others' feelings towards us would help all of us deal with the
insecurities: they are natural rather than fatal.

There are also some workers (Lewis and McAvoy 1984; Orford
and O'Reilly 1981; Platt and Labate 1976) who show that drug
abuse and alcohol abuse are sometimes means by which certain types
of people deal with the problem of uncomfortable relationships –
and thereby provide themselves with a handy "self-handicapping
strategy" (that is to say, a self-created problem that provides an
apparently valid reason for the collapse of their relationships). It is
more acceptable to people to blame the inadequate development of
relationships on their use of drugs or alcohol, for example, than to
have to blame it directly on themselves as people.

Dealing with sexual dysfunction and enhancing intimacy

In some cases an individual has no trouble in being affiliative, no
trouble in developing relationships, and no difficulties in feeling
intimate toward others but has functional or psychological problems
when it comes to sexual and other intimate behaviors. In such cases,
again, the reparative techniques are a mixture of attention to the
individual's problems and those that result from the interaction or
interplay of the two persons in their intimate behavior with one
another. Masters and Johnson (1970), for example, claim to have
dealt fairly successfully with such hypophilia (reduced or inappro-
priately low sexual drive or achievement), and to have done so by
several techniques of having one partner service the other person's
pleasure needs. In part their work seems to succeed by reducing

anxiety, but several other researchers (e.g. Yaffe 1981) report that there is also a skill-training element, including the assertiveness skills necessary to initiate or decline sexual interaction.

Another part of the problem may be that the couple does not communicate intimate feelings in an adequately expressive way. Neimeyer and Hudson (1985) have developed some "living laboratory" methods for couples that help to improve their intimate interactions with one another, while Miell (1984) has indicated the ways in which self-disclosure in pairs may be strategically enhanced in order to increase the couple's intimacy. R. A. Lewis (1978) also showed how intimacy training can be used to improve a couple's experiences of one another, in research focused on intimacy between pairs of male friends. All such methods work by improving the efficiency of the expression of emotion and therefore by clarifying the couple's feelings for each other in positive, enhancing ways. Under this heading, then, we are dealing with the repair of relationships where the partners want to get together and where the problem is essentially the result of one person's habitual social difficulty which is either inherent or generated by the psychological reaction to the partner.

Intrapsychic phase and intrapsychic repair

By contrast, the intrapsychic phase of relationship breakdown is, as we saw in Chapter 6, a complaining/moaning/griping/dissatisfaction stage where the only form of repair that matters is making one person feel more positive about the partner. It is essentially a cognitive phase where beliefs about the partner and the relationship are at issue. The relevant techniques, therefore, will repair the problem by dealing with the person's negative beliefs and trying to change them (Duck 1984a). J. Wright and Fichten (1976) and Fichten and Wright (1985) have indicated that unhappy partners attribute blame unequally and tend to see their partner as responsible for all the conflicts in a relationship. It is unlikely that such a one-sided view is ever accurate and these authors videotaped discussions between the partners in the hope of removing the biases in perception and attribution that exist in the relationship. Other techniques involve the complainer in listing the positive and pleasing qualities of the partner (Bandura 1977), or having the person keep a diary recording the nice things that the partner does. Yet another possibility is to encourage the

person to reinterpret the partner's behavior in a positive light
("positive altercasting": Miller and Parks 1982), or to get the person
to reflect on the negative feelings of himself or herself and to reassess,
therefore, the costs created for the partner in the relationship. Any
reassessment of the balance of equity in the relationship will make
the person realize that things are not entirely one-sided (Hatfield and
Traupmann 1981). Any forced recording of one's own negative
inputs to the relationship encourages the person to consider the
partner's perspective and thereby reach a more balanced and objective view of the complaints made about the partner. This should
encourage the individual to take account of that partner's reasonable
defenses against the complaints.

Dyadic stage and dyadic solutions

Perhaps the most difficult phase of break-up is that point where both
people realize that there are problems and begin to argue. A person
who comments on another's performance of relational interaction is
setting himself or herself up for some stormy reactions. As we have
repeatedly seen in various ways, it is not socially acceptable to
comment either on non-verbal behavior or on the state of a relationship. To comment on the performance of communication or
relating in a partnership is to break several conventions and is clearly
unfamiliar for most people. For those reasons we find that partners
having relationship problems not only find the discussions themselves hurtful (Baxter 1982) but also find the sheer expression of
tension difficult and something that becomes a management issue in
its own right (Kaplan 1976). A characteristic style of behavior in
conflicts like this is that partners develop a cross-complaining cycle
("You did this," "Well you did this," "Well that's because you do
this," and so on). Each party counters a complaint with one of his or
her own instead of taking the partner's complaint as if it were a
reasonable viewpoint to have (Gottman 1979). In short, the partners
act as if they do not respect each other's different perspectives, and
that makes it even harder for their views to be reconciled.

At this point we are therefore concerned with the process of dyadic
interaction. The whole business of dealing with the occurrence of a
hurtful argument is a hard one, over and above the content of the
argument and what it means to the couple (Duck 1984b). Sometimes
it causes more hurt than anything that is said. At other times, the

sheer expression of conflict can be good for couples and can clear the air, for which reason it has been strongly advocated by Kaplan (1984). However, its unskilled or unguided use can be problematic and counselors therefore usually speak to the partners separately before having them discuss their problems together.

Social support and the social phase

The social network serves many unobtrusive functions in the repair or dissolution of relationships (Cobb and Jones-Cobb 1984; LaGaipa 1982). At some points it serves to sustain the person going through a crisis in a key relationship and we have already seen what can be done for an individual by means of advice, gossip, and subtle attacks on the other person's version of events. Support and repairing can also be provided by means of "intervention teams" (LaGaipa 1982) which try to give the couple some help in sorting themselves out. In some cases couple therapy or couple intervention is essential; for example Arkowitz et al. (1982) have shown that depressed persons' partners often need guidance on how to conduct interaction with the depressed person. The first role of the networks is therefore to keep the couple together by means of intervention teams that try to engineer a more harmonious climate through talking to the partners separately and together, reminding them of their obligations to social norms, and urging them to react to social pressures as well as to their own feelings about each other (LaGaipa 1982). There is a considerable amount of "networking" done at this point, with network members talking to one another in attempts to muster support to sustain the relationship. If that attempt is seen to flounder, however, the network's role as relational repairer changes in a number of ways. First, it focuses on repairing the individuals separately, by the gossipy, feuding means referred to in Chapter 6 and discussed more fully in Boissevain (1974). Second, it helps by the provision of "lay treatment networks" (Gottlieb 1976), whether these are community caregivers such as the clergy, or organized self-help groups, like Parents Without Partners. Pilisuk and Minkler (1980) also showed how isolated or separated people could be relationally repaired (or prepared for relationships) by joining voluntary organizations which have the incidental effect of providing opportunities for further relationships and so help a person to recover from the loss of a previous relationship. Thus, although the roles of networks in repair may be varied or multifarious (Gottlieb 1976), it is clear that the social phase of repair is a significant one.

Grave digging, grave dressing, and return from the grave

Research is now increasingly exploring one of the toughest but most enduring parts of relationship dissolution, namely the period when partners get over the break. Weber (1983) has reported on the way in which identity management is accomplished in leaving a relationship and the ways in which the partners repair their own self-concepts and their future in relationships. As Weber *et al.* (1988) have suggested, the story time in relationship repair is significant as much for the attitudes that it creates for future relationships as for its contribution to the understanding of the past. The role of the grave dressing phase in the repair of ex-partners is probably one of the most exciting areas that remains for future work to explore.

Summary

The repair of relationships can mean the repair of the individuals in a relationship, the repair of the mechanics of the relationship, or the repair of the person after he or she has left the relationship. This chapter has explored the ways in which the various parts of relationship repair interrelate and serve to enhance a relationship, stabilize it, or satisfactorily extract individuals from unsatisfactory relationships so that they can cast their eyes to the future and new relationships which do not have the same problems as the one they have left.

Further reading

Christensen, A. (1983). Intervention. In H. H. Kelley, Berscheid E., Christensen, A., Harvey, J. H., Huston, T. L., Levinger, G., McClintock, E., Peplau, L. A., and Peterson, D. R. *Close Relationships*. New York: Freeman. A very comprehensive and thoughtful chapter on interventions for distressed relationships of many different sorts.
Duck, S. W. (ed.) (1984). *Personal Relationships 5: Repairing Personal Relationships*. London and New York: Academic Press. An edited collec-

tion of papers addressing several different sides of the problem of repairing relationships, whether distressed marital relationships, relationships disturbed by drug abuse, or general approaches to relational repair. The book also contains chapters on the role of social support in repairing people and their relationships, and chapters dealing with the healing role of good physician–patient relationships and general therapy of relationships.

Filsinger, E. E. and Lewis, R. A. (1981). *Assessing Marriage: New Behavioral Approaches*. Beverly Hills, CA: Sage. An edited collection of papers describing and critiquing the latest advances in behavioral assessments of marriage, drawing on psychology, sociology, and family studies.

8 / OVERVIEW

This book ought to surprise those social psychologists whose views of the area of friendship and personal relationships were shaped by their memories of the work on attraction to strangers. Such research was abundant in the 1960s and 1970s and that image of the field is retained by many who considered it in that era, became discouraged, and went on to study other topics. The field of personal relationships, by contrast with this heritage, is so fundamentally different from the field of interpersonal attraction ten years ago that it deals with topics alien to many memories and does so in a way that is also alien to most recollections of the then-prevailing laboratory methodology. This chapter will consider those major changes and in doing so draws heavily on a paper which I wrote with Harriet Sants (Duck and Sants 1983).

As indicated throughout the book, the emphasis of the best current research on relating to others is cross-disciplinary and process-oriented; it stresses the behavioral components of relating in the everyday lives of relational participants in addition to pure cognition, attitudes, or attribution; and it has a place for the interpersonal communication through which many relational processes actually operate. It focuses on the strategies and communicative social devices that real people use in real, everyday contexts to achieve real relational goals. It emphasizes the non-automatic nature of relating, its two-sidedness (as distinct from the one-sided impression-formation and judgemental emphasis of much previous work) and its embeddedness in the extensive span of people's real lives and social contexts. As such I think the work has, by incorporating more than social psychology, become truly social and will continue to develop as such.

The reasons for these improvements are to be found in the rejection of four unwanted heirlooms inherited from the four ancestors of the study of relationships: interpersonal attraction, the social psychology of impression formation, attribution theory, and the debates about similarity-complementarity of personality (see Chapter 2). According to Duck and Sants (1983), the four unwanted heirlooms have led to a predominance of a view that de-emphasizes the continuous, processual nature of relationships and tends to depict them as states. Marcel Proust once observed that although life is always in motion, humans find it convenient to see it as snapshot stills. The tendency of researchers to view the continuities of relationships as if they were still/steady states seems to be a part of this human tendency, as is the tendency for people in relationships to focus on key "events" and "turning-points" as one-off things rather than occurrences embedded in a continuously moving stream of experience.

The tendency is a very real psychological tool, however, and in social psychology it seems to derive from these four heirlooms.

1 Relationships as the chemistry of partner attributes, that is the erroneous view (discussed in Chapters 3 and 4) that the satisfactory development of a relationship between two people can be predicted from knowledge of their personal characteristics as individuals. Social scientists are human, too, and are influenced by the times in which they live: the predominance of the view that people make better partners when they match on personal characteristics once permeated psychological theorizing and to some extent still does. "Common sense" provides the basis for many scientific views and it surely takes the position that relationships are predictable (and that the success of relationships is predictable) from the individual characteristics that two people take with them into the relationship before they meet.

2 Relationships as undigested interactions, that is the erroneous assumptions, discussed at several points in this book, that people do not ponder about interactions that have happened, or will happen, do not plan or reminisce, and do not reformulate their understandings of "what really happened." The assumption has often been that the behavior in an interaction is all that counts and that people's strategies, intentions, plans, and reminiscences or

retrospections have little to do with it, despite their vast contribution to human experience.

3 Relationships as crocks of gold at the end of the rainbow, that is the erroneous assumption implicit in some of the research discussed throughout this book that "a relationship" is a clear and clearly observable entity that we could bottle and study in the laboratory if we could only identify it. Rather we should be realizing that a relationship emerges from interaction and from people's thoughts about interaction (Burnett *et al.* 1987).

4 Relaters as air traffic controllers, that is the erroneous belief noted in Chapters 2–7 that human beings are in perfect control of their actions, that they do everything thinkingly, that when they process information they do so entirely rationally, that they can hold enormous amounts of relevant detail at their fingertips, and that they are constantly self-aware and competent. This is different from point (2) above, which argues that people occasionally make plans and have forethought, however misleading or erroneous or mistaken it turns out to be.

Do relationships result from the chemistry of partner attributes?

At first blush, a reasonable assumption is that successful relationships between people are predictable from their "entry characteristics" – for instance, the personality attributes or looks that partners bring with them to the relationship. As I showed earlier, the search for the magically influential characteristic or the magically effective type of matching between characteristics was ultimately quite unproductive as long as it assumed the absolute effects of such factors and took no account of the ways in which they actually operated in the social and communicative behavior of real life. By assessing "objective" personality similarity or "objective" physical attractiveness, the experimental studies unintentionally short-circuited the very personal, subjective, and individual reactions to such cues which really were the very stuff that they were trying to assess. Not only that, but also they emasculated the social processes that are important in effecting whatever influences such cues have in real life. We should rather have been asking how people behave when they detect that they are similar, and how that is different from the way they behave when they detect that they are different. We should also have been asking how liking for another person can be increased by encouraging people to search actively for similarities. By contrast investigators have merely provided instance of similarities and dissimilarities and assessed subjects' reactions – thereby circumventing the very interesting and important process by which subject habitually detect similarities and dissimilarities in normal life. In real life we do not know about our similarities to someone else so directly; rather, we have to make inferences and deductions in the context of the real life demands and behaviors of others (which often include the deliberate concealment of attitudes and beliefs). The detection of similarities and the assessment of their significance are not easy tasks in the hurly-burly of real life. Accordingly, such similarities and differences have their effects not by reason of their objective qualities but through their interpersonal consequences as the more recent research described in this book makes increasingly clear.

As I have shown in Chapters 2–4 here, the relevance of partner characteristics is not to be found in the places where it was assumed to be; partners do not simply match up like parts of a jigsaw and then *automatically* discover that a vibrant relationship is an inevitable consequence. Rather, there are two ways in which a person's characteristics have an effect. First, in the way in which such measurable personality characteristics translate into specific relational behaviors in daily life that influence partners' interactions with one another; and second, in the way in which people discover and communicate about one another's characteristics (and incidentally the characteristics of third parties, since gossip about others serves a very important bonding function in everyday social life).

It is quite clear that, as Duck and Sants (1983: 32) put it:

> the mere juxtaposition of two partners' attributes does not create a relationship. . . . Active social processes do this, the social processes of negotiating, communicating "deep" personal attributes, and creating behavioral consequences of them.

Fortunately for the field, researchers are beginning to explore these important social, interpersonal, and negotiative processes. Lloyd and Cate (1985), Kelly *et al.* (1985), and Surra (1987) have all shown the ways in which the organization of the tiny parts of everyday life influence relationships and the ways that such structuring of the nuts-and-bolts of the relationship acquires its significance as distinct from the flat influences of personality, attitudes, and cognition. Also important is the sequencing and timing of such interactive processes – filter theorists were right about that – and, as Duck and Sants (1983) suggest, the analogy is to the mixing of water with concentrated sulphuric acid. Whichever way the mixing is done, the result is dilute sulphuric acid; but if the water is poured into the acid there is also violent and dangerous spitting, while the other way of doing things produces only a gentle warming. Even if theorists adhere to the idea that the mixing of attributes is influential to relationships, we need to do more careful work to clarify the means by which the mixing is best achieved in real social lives and we should not assume that there are simple and equally balanced effects of any order or method of achieving the mix. In everyday relationships, partners carry out a great deal of negotiating and compromising as well as simply being impressed by and attracted by each other. Even if initial attraction causes the coming together of two possible partners on the basis of their relative or absolute characteristics, that by itself can never make a working, living relationship.

Are relationships simply undigested interactions?

One of the points that I have stressed throughout this book is the notion that people sometimes think about what they do and sometimes act unthinkingly, or carelessly, or on the basis of mistaken beliefs or understandings. However, in significant relationships I have no doubt (although I have no formal evidence yet, either!) that people typically think about such relationships, about their partner, about interactions they have had, about future interactions, about future directions for the relationship, about their feelings about it all and much else besides, at least from time to time. When they do so, it has consequences for that relationship and these can be major behavioral consequences such as the plucking up of courage to ask someone out on a date, the decision to file for divorce, the intent to confront a friend about a relational misdemeanor, and so on.

Hinde (1981) has pointed out that one interaction influences another in relationships – what I do now with you will set a scene for what we do together later – and relationships, like life in general, are built on previous experiences and past history. However, what I think now about you can also influence what we do, both now and in the future (Duck 1980a). Thus the two partners' thoughts about the

relationship and its future will create the context for their interactions (Burnett 1986), will establish the general strategies that they
use in the interactions, and will provide the basis for the assessments
of their success or failure in achieving those objectives. Hence we can
experience disappointment, regret, remorse, or elation, which in
their own ways are all the emotional or psychological consequences
of matching our achievements with our intentions.

The interpretative digestion of interactions, then, seems to me to
be a key aspect of the relational enterprise, and researchers should
not assume that "the relationship" is a product of interaction or
behavior alone; rather, it emerges from the thinking that the two
partners do in relation to those interactions (see Burnett *et al.* 1987).
Relationships, then (as distinct from interactions, interaction
sequences, and interaction patterns), are mental associations
between people as much as they are behavioral associations, and are
historically derived representations of experience as much as they are
interpersonally communicative entities. We have a relationship if we
both think that we have one and can construct a mental history of it.
As previously noted, such thinking is important not only because it
creates a narrative for the previous development of the relationship
but also because it creates an expected future for it and thereby
provides both a context for its continuing development and a subtle
form of routine: things will continue, for the time being at least, as
they are. The stories that we tell now about the relationship in the
past are stories with implications for the future. It is important for
future work on relationships to explore the role of such narratives in
the creation of the sense of "being in a relationship" that makes such
a substantial contribution to the existence of the relationship
(Gergen and Gergen 1987). Such a view might also help us to eschew
the rather naive general assumption that retrospective accounts of
relational events are necessarily and merely "biased." If it is true that
retrospections are biased, it is certainly also true that researchers
have not yet clarified with any certainty the nature, form, and
predictable patterns of such biases. On the other hand, I prefer to
believe that "bias" here is a rather interesting psychological
phenomenon and one that will repay the attention that researchers
should be devoting to it. I argued earlier that memory for social
experience is relevant to the entering of relationships (see Chapter 1).
Equally the processes by which we reconstruct and remember the
past of our relationships make a fascinating topic. Miell (1987) has
already shown that a person's memory for the distant past of a

relationship or for its general pattern is significantly influenced by the
very recent experiences in the relationship. Duck and Pond (1988)
have also indicated that the remembering of first meetings is actually
negotiated between partners rather than being a simple historical
depiction. Memory for relationships and relationship events or
processes, like history itself, is rarely a simple photographic record:
in any case, photographs, whether in albums or in the mind, can be
retouched. Retrospective accounts of relationships, as of other
things, are likely, I believe, to be subject to systematic alteration to
meet current relationship and personal needs. Our task in future
should be to gain understanding of how retrospective accounts differ
from present experience or future expectations or contemporary
accounts of the same things, since the differences are surely psychologically informative, not merely indicative of error. In coming to
understand changes in accounts we shall, I believe, come to
understand some key psychological processes that drive relational
experience.

Are relationships "crocks of gold at the end of the rainbow"?

The crock of gold at the end of the rainbow is an illusory item since
the rainbow's end moves as the observer moves, and it is therefore
never reached. Relationships are similar in that their substance
changes with the perspective of the observer (Olson 1977), which is
one important reason why researchers need to be careful before
assuming that their view of a relationship is the only one or the only
one which is correct. If partners think about relationships and can
plan them or develop strategies for coping with them, they may each
reach utterly different conclusions about the success of an interaction
and even about the nature of the relationship, despite the fact that, in
some other sense, they were in the same relationship and had the
same experience. This is not so much a problem for the relationship
or for researchers as a fundamental fact of relational and human life
(Duck and Sants 1983; Olson 1977), and one that we do not yet
sufficiently understand.

Future work on relationships will clearly need to explore the ways
in which relational perspectives differ and what this means for the
description of the relationship, both in scientific and in personal
terms. Clearly the creation (by partners) of a jointly accepted account

of the relationship is an important part of its existence, yet the evidence seems to be that partners do not agree on fundamental aspects of the relationship such as the time when the first intercourse occurred (Surra 1987; see also Chapter 7) and where they first met (Duck and Miell 1986). A partnership in which one person claims that they met in a coffee bar and the other claims that they met at a lecture may both assert confidently fifteen weeks later that they met just as one of them was going from a coffee bar to a lecture (cf. Duck and Miell 1986). As researchers we need to explore the meaning of such divergence and subsequent convergence of narratives in the creation of the sense of being in a relationship and we need to dispense with our present assumption that both partners will agree with one another and with us as researchers unless they are somehow "biased" or "wrong."

We need also to be circumspect and cautious before assuming that the insiders will necessarily agree with outsiders who witness the relationship. Particularly during relationship distress, people go to a lot of trouble to conceal the dynamics of their relationship from the outside world, but the very fact that observers may characterize a relationship in one way and the partners in another is an interesting phenomenon that may or may not indicate erroneous perception. I doubt that the two partners will agree with an "objective" observer about all aspects of their relationship. Once again, the existence of such discrepancies and differences is not merely an irritating problem for researchers, so much as a profound truth about relating to others, and a truth that we should seek to comprehend more fully.

As students of relationships our interest must lie in the psychological interior of relationships – how they feel or seem to their members, and how those interiors change – rather than simply with the external observables of the partners' interactions together. We should also be concerned with the ways in which the interior aspects of the relationships are communicated to others, whether it be the partner or other persons, as a function of the views that the people have of their relationship.

Are relaters really "air traffic controllers"?

The common view of air traffic controllers is that they are perfectly rational beings capable of processing vast amounts of information under extreme stress and nevertheless getting it right most of the time, whatever is going on around them. The mistake still made in much literature on relationships is precisely that we assume too easily that information processing is rational and intelligent in relationships when much of the time our subjects and our own personal lives reveal that it is not so. People are naturally confused and puzzled about life and it is time we recognized that in our formal theorizing (Duck 1986). Not only do normal human beings experience normal human doubts and anxieties about many things, including their relationships, but also, as a natural part of normal human life, they are subject to conflicting advice and pressures, in the context of which the advantages of one kind of behavior over another must be assessed. Sometimes human behavior has unforeseen consequences and very often our control or influence over a relationship is much less than perfect, so that even if we were perfectly rational, logical information processors, our rationality may be undermined by the unpredictable actions of a relational partner.

The research on attribution and social cognition often seems to me to represent human beings as the kinds of people we would like to be rather than the kinds of people we really are. In relationships, as elsewhere in life, I do not see people being optimally efficient or on top of everything. We all make mistakes and are thoughtless or inconsiderate or sometimes too busy. Rather than relegating such occurrences to mere "costs" in a relational equation, it is time that we began to understand the chaos in relationships and the flops as well as the strategic successes. No one has a perfectly successful and satisfactory relational life, not even an air traffic controller.

So . . .

The field of research in personal relationships is about to witness a major boom that will take us comfortably into the next millenium. In order to make the best possible progress at such a time, researchers have to make the kinds of fundamental changes to their approach to the study of relationships that are indicated above. In twenty years we shall look back on a field that has made substantial contributions to the understanding of everyday human and social and communicative life precisely because that, at last, is what it has begun to study.

Further reading

Burnett, R. and Clarke, D. D. (1988) *Thinking about Relationships*. London: Methuen. One of the New Wave of books in this field which explores relationships from a new angle, looking at the role of accounting and awareness in relationships.

Burnett, R., McGhee, P., and Clarke, D. D. (eds) (1987). *Accounting for Relationships: Explanation, Representation and Knowledge*. London: Methuen. An edited collection of papers on the role of language, thought, and knowledge in the conduct of relationships. This book is important because it is the first to give comprehensive coverage of the role of language, communication, and social cognition in relationships and tie them explicitly to the conduct of relationships.

Duck, S. W. and Sants, H. K. A. (1983). On the origin of the specious: Are personal relationships really interpersonal states? *Journal of Social and Clinical Psychology*, 1, 27–41. The original paper on which the present chapter is based.

Journal of Social and Personal Relationships, 1984– . The only journal dealing with this new field exclusively, and one where the most recent research at the cutting edge is to be found.

Perlman, D. and Duck, S. W. (eds) (1987). *Intimate Relationships: Development, Dynamics, and Deterioration*. Beverly Hills, CA: Sage. An edited collection of original papers on the nature of intimacy and the growth and decline of intimate relationships. Chapters include discussion of relationships after divorce, the role of self-monitoring in relationships, and jealousy in intimate relations.

REFERENCES

Acitelli, L. K. and Duck, S. W. (1987). Intimacy as the proverbial elephant. In D. Perlman and S. W. Duck (eds) *Intimate Relationships: Development, Dynamics, and Deterioration.* Beverly Hills, CA: Sage.

Adams, J. S. (1965). Inequity in social exchange. In L. Berkowitz (ed.), *Advances in Experimental Social Psychology*, vol. 2. New York: Academic Press.

Adelman, M. (1987). Love's urban agent: Social support and the matchmaker. Paper to Iowa Conference on Personal Relationships, University of Iowa, May–June.

Adler, A. (1929/1959). *Understanding Human Nature.* New York: Premier Books.

Adler, T. and Furman, W. (1988). A model for children's relationships and relationship dysfunctions. In S. W. Duck, D. F. Hay, S. E. Hobfoll, W. Ickes and B. M. Montgomery (eds) *Handbook of Personal Relationships.* Chichester: Wiley.

Ahrons, C. and Rodgers, R. (1987). *Divorced Families.* New York: Norton.

Ainsworth, M. D. S., Blehar, M. C., Waters, E., and Wall, S. (1978). *Patterns of Attachment. A psychological study of the strange situation.* Hillsdale, NJ: Lawrence Erlbaum.

Alicke, M. D., Smith R. H., and Klotz, M. L. (1986). Judgements of physical attractiveness: The role of faces and bodies. *Personality and Social Psychology Bulletin*, **12**, 381–9.

Altman, I. and Taylor, D. A. (1973). *Social Penetration: The Development of Interpersonal Relationships.* New York: Holt, Rinehart & Winston.

Altman, I., Vinsel, A., and Brown, B. B. (1981). Dialectic conceptions in social psychology: An application to social penetration and privacy regulation. In L. Berkowitz (ed.) *Advances in Experimental Social Psychology.* New York: Academic Press.

Argyle, M. (1983). *The Psychology of Interpersonal Behaviour*, 4th edn. Harmondsworth: Penguin.

(1987). *The Psychology of Happiness*. London: Methuen.

Argyle, M. and Henderson, M. (1984). The rules of friendship. *Journal of Social and Personal Relationships*, 1, 211–37.

(1985a). The rules of relationships. In S. W. Duck and D. Perlman (eds), *Understanding Personal Relationships: An Interdisciplinary Approach*. London: Sage.

(1985b). *The Anatomy of Relationships*. London: Methuen.

Arkowitz, H., Holliday, S., and Hutter, M. (1982). Depressed women and their husbands: A study of marital interaction and adjustment. Paper presented at the Annual Meeting of the Association for the Advancement of Behavior Therapy, Los Angeles.

Athanasiou, R. and Sarkin, R. (1974). Premarital sexual behavior and postmarital adjustment. *Archives of Sexual Behavior*, 3, 207–25.

Ayres, J. (1983). Strategies to maintain relationships: Their identification and perceived usage. *Communication Quarterly*, 31, 62–7.

Ball, R. E. and Robbins, L. (1984). Marital status and life satisfaction of Black men. *Journal of Social and Personal Relationships*, 1, 459–70.

Bandura, A. (1977). *Social Learning Theory*. Englewood Cliffs, NJ: Prentice-Hall.

Barnes, J. A. (1972). *Social Networks*. Reading, MA: Addison-Wesley.

Baxter, L. A. (1982). Strategies for ending relationships: Two studies. *Western Journal of Speech Communication*, 46, 223–41.

(1984). Trajectories of relationship disengagement. *Journal of Social and Personal Relationships*, 1, 29–48.

(1985). Accomplishing relationship disengagement. In S. W. Duck and D. Perlman (eds) *Understanding Personal Relationships: An Interdisciplinary Approach*. London: Sage.

(1986). Gender differences in the heterosexual relationship rules embedded in break-up accounts. *Journal of Social and Personal Relationships*, 3, 289–306.

(1987). Symbols of relationship identity in relationship cultures. *Journal of Personal and Social Relationships*, 4, 261–80.

Baxter, L. A. and Bullis, C. (1986). Turning points in developing romantic relationships. *Human Communication Research*, 12, 469–93.

Baxter, L. A. and Wilmot, W. (1984). Secret tests: Social strategies for acquiring information about the state of the relationship. *Human Communication Research*, 11, 171–201.

(1985). Taboo topics in close relationships. *Journal of Social and Personal Relationships*, 2, 253–69.

(1986). Interaction characteristics of disengaging, stable, and growing relationships. In R. Gilmour and S. W. Duck (eds) *The Emerging Field of Personal Relationships*. Hillsdale, NJ: Lawrence Erlbaum.

Beck, W. H., Ward-Hull, C. I., and McLear, P. M. (1976). Variables related to women's somantic preferences of the male and female body. *Journal of Personality and Social Psychology*, 34, 1,200–10.

Bell, R. A. and Daly, J. A. (1984). The affinity-seeking function of communication. *Communication Monographs*, 51, 91–115.

Bentler, P. M. and Newcomb, M. D. (1978). Longitudinal study of marital success and failure. *Journal of Consulting and Clinical Psychology*, 46, 1,053–70.

Berg, J. H. and Clark, M. S. (1986). Differences in social exchange between intimate and other relationships: Gradually evolving or quickly apparent? In V. J. Derlega and B. A. Winstead (eds) *Friendship and Social Interaction*. New York: Springer-Verlag.

Berger, C. R. (1988). Uncertainty and information exchange in developing relationships. In S. W. Duck, D. F. Hay, S. E. Hobfoll, W. Ickes and B. M. Montgomery (eds) *Handbook of Personal Relationships*. Chichester: Wiley.

Berger, C. R. and Bradac, J. J. (1982). *Language and Social Knowledge: Uncertainty in Interpersonal Relations*. London: Edward Arnold.

Berscheid, E. (1981). An overview of the psychological effects of physical attractiveness. In G. W. Lucker, K. A. Ribbens, and J. A. McNamara, Jr. (eds) *Psychological Aspects of Facial Form*. Michigan: CHGD.

(1985). Interpersonal attraction. In G. Lindzey and E. Aronson (eds) *Handbook of Social Psychology*, vol. 2, 3rd end. New York: Random House.

Berscheid, E. and Walster, E. H. (1974) A little bit about love. In T. L. Huston (ed.) *Foundations of Interpersonal Attraction*. New York: Academic Press.

(1978). *Interpersonal Attraction*, 2nd edn. Reading, MA: Addison-Wesley.

Blankenship, V., Hnat, S. M., Hess, T. G., and Brown, D. R. (1984) Reciprocal interaction and similarity of personal attributes. *Journal of Social and Personal Relationships*, 1, 415–32.

Bloom, B., Asher, S. J., and White, S. W. (1978). Marital disruption as a stressor: A review and analysis. *Psychological Bulletin*, 85, 867–94.

Blumstein, P. and Schwartz, P. (1983). *American Couples: Money, Work, Sex*. New York: William Morrow.

Boissevain, J. (1974). *Friends of Friends: Networks, Manipulators and Coalitions*. Oxford: Blackwell.

Bradac, J. (1983). Social knowledge in relationships. Paper presented at International Conference on Language and Social Behaviour, Bristol, July.

Braiker, H. B. and Kelley, H. H. (1979). Conflict in the development of close relationships. In R. L. Burgess and T. L. Huston (eds) *Social Exchange in Developing Relationships*. New York: Academic Press.

Brown, G. W. and Harris, T. (1978). *Social Origins of Depression: A Study of Psychiatric Disorder in Women*. London: Tavistock.

Burgoon, J. K. and Koper, R. J. (1984). Nonverbal and relational communication associated with reticence. *Human Communication Research*, 10, 601–26.

Burnett, R. (1986). Conceptualisation of personal relationships. Unpublished D. Phil. thesis, University of Oxford UK.

(1987). Reflection on personal relationships. In R. Burnett, P. McGhee, and D. D. Clarke (eds) *Accounting for Relationships: Explanation, Representation and Knowledge*. London: Methuen.

Burnett, R. and Clarke, D. D. (1988). *Thinking about Relationships*. London: Methuen.

Burnett, R., McGhee, P., and Clarke, D. D. (eds) (1987). *Accounting for Relationships: Explanation, Representation and Knowledge*. London: Methuen.

Bush, C. R., Bush, J., and Jennings, J. (1988) Effects of jealousy threats on relationship perceptions and emotions. *Journal of Social and Personal Relationships*, 5, 285–303.

Byrne, D. (1961). Interpersonal attraction and attitude similarity. *Journal of Abnormal and Social Psychology*, 62, 713–15.

(1969). Attitudes and attraction. In L. Berkowitz (ed.) *Advances in Experimental Social Psychology*, vol. 4. New York: Academic Press.

(1971). *The Attraction Paradigm*. New York: Academic Press.

Byrne, D. and Lamberth, J. (1971). Cognitive and reinforcement theory as complementary approaches to the study of attraction. In B. I. Murstein (ed.) *Theories of Attraction and Love*. New York: Springer.

Byrne, D., Nelson, D., and Reeves, K. (1966). The effects of consensual validation and invalidation on attraction as a function of verifiability. *Journal of Experimental Social Psychology*, 2, 98–107.

Cahn, D. (1987). *Letting Go: A Practical Theory of Relationship Disengagement and Re-engagement*. Albany, NY: SUNY Press.

Cameron, C., Oskamp, S., and Sparks, W. (1977). Courtship American style: Newspaper ads. *The Family Coordinator*, 26, 27–30.

Carnegie, D. (1936). *How to Win Friends and Influence People*. Fortune: New York.

Cate, R. M. and Lloyd, S. A. (1988). Courtship. In S. W. Duck, D. F. Hay, S. E. Hobfoll, W. Ickes and B. M. Montgomery (eds) *Handbook of Personal Relationships*. Chichester: Wiley.

Cate, R. M., Henton, J., Koval, J., Christopher, F. S., and Lloyd, S. A. (1982). Premarital abuse: A social psychological perspective. *Journal of Family Issues*, 3, 79–90.

Cate, R. M., Lloyd, S. A., Henton, M. M., and Larson, J. H. (1982). Fairness and reward level as predictors of relationship satisfaction. *Social Psychology Quarterly*, 45, 177–81.

Cattell, H. and Nesselroade, J. R. (1967). Likeness and completeness theories examined by sixteen personality factor measures on stable and unstable married couples. *Journal of Personality and Social Psychology*, 7, 351–61.

Cheal, D. (1986). The social dimensions of gift behavior. *Journal of Social and Personal Relationships*, 3, 423–40.

Christensen, A. (1983). Intervention. In H. H. Kelley, E. Berscheid, A. Christensen, J. H. Harvey, T. L. Huston, G. Levinger, E. McClintock, L. A. Peplau, and D. R. Peterson. *Close Relationships*. New York: Freeman.

Christopher, F. S. and Cate, R. M. (1982). Factors involved in premarital sexual decision-making. Paper presented at International Conference on Personal Relations, Madison.

(1985). Premarital sexual pathways and relationship development. *Journal of Social and Personal Relationships*, 2, 271–88.

Clarke, D. D., Allen, C. M. B., and Salinas, M. (1986). Conjoint time-budgeting: Investigating behavioral accommodation in marriage. *Journal of Social and Personal Relationships*, 3, 53–70.

Cobb, S. (1976). Social support as a moderator of life stress. *Psychosomatic Medicine*, 38, 300–14.

Cobb, S. and Jones-Cobb, J. (1984). Social support, support groups and marital relationships. In S. W. Duck (ed.) *Personal Relationships 5: Repairing Personal Relationships*. London and New York: Academic Press.

Comadena, M. (1982). Accuracy in detecting deception: Intimate and friendship relationships. In M. Burgoon (ed.) *Communication Yearbook*, vol. 6. Beverly Hills, CA: Sage.

Cortez, C. (1986). Relationships with media anchors. Unpublished manuscript, University of Iowa.

Davis, J. D. (1978). When boy meets girl: Sex roles and the negotiation of intimacy in an acquaintance exercise. *Journal of Personality and Social Psychology*, 36, 684–92.

Davis, K. E. and Latty-Mann, H. (1987) Love styles and relationship quality: A contribution to validation. *Journal of Social and Personal Relationships*, 4, 409–27.

Davis, K. E. and Todd, M. (1985) Assessing friendship: Prototypes, paradigm cases and relationship description. In S. W. Duck and D. Perlman (eds) *Understanding Personal Relationships: An Interdisciplinary Approach*. London: Sage.

Davis, M. H. and Franzoi, S. L. (1986). Adolescent loneliness, self-disclosure and private self-consciousness: A longitudinal investigation. *Journal of Personality and Social Psychology*, 51, 595–608.

Day, B. R. (1961). A comparison of personality needs of courtship couples and same-sex friends. *Sociology and Social Research*, 45, 435–40.

Deal, J. E. and Wampler, K. S. (1986). Dating violence: The primacy of previous experience. *Journal of Social and Personal Relationships*, 3, 457–71.

Delia, J. G. (1980). Some tentative thoughts concerning the study of interpersonal relationships and their development. *Western Journal of Speech Communication*, 44, 97–103.

Derlega, V. J. (1984). Self-disclosure and intimate relationships. In V. J.

Derlega (ed.) *Communication, Intimacy, and Close Relationships*. New York: Academic Press.

Derlega, V. J. and Winstead, B. A. (eds) (1986). *Friendship and Social Interaction*. New York: Springer-Verlag.

Derlega, V. J., Winstead, B. A., Wong, P. T. P., and Hunter, S. (1985). Gender effects in an initial encounter: A case where men exceed women in disclosure. *Journal of Social and Personal Relationships*, 2, 25–44.

Dickens, W. J. and Perlman, D. (1981). Friendship over the life-cycle. In S. W. Duck and R. Gilmour (eds) *Personal Relationships 2: Developing Personal Relationships*. London: Academic Press.

Dillard, J. P. and Miller, K. (1988) Intimate relationships in task environments. In S. W. Duck, D. F. Hay, S. E. Hobfoll, W. Ickes and B. M. Montgomery (eds) *Handbook of Personal Relationships*. Chichester: Wiley.

Dindia, K. and Baxter, L. A. (1987). Maintenance and repair strategies in marital relationships. *Journal of Social and Personal Relationships*, 4, 143–58.

Dion, K. K. (1972). Physical attractiveness and evaluation of children's transgressions. *Journal of Personality and Social Psychology*, 24, 207–13.

Dion, K. K., Berscheid, E., and Walster, E. H. (1972). What is beautiful is good. *Journal of Personality and Social Psychology*, 24, 285–90.

Douglas, W. (1985). Anticipated interaction and information seeking. *Human Communication Research*, 12, 243–58.

(1987). Affinity-testing in initial interaction. *Journal of Social and Personal Relationships*, 4, 3–16.

Driscoll, R., Davis, K. E., and Lipetz, M. E. (1972). Parental interference and romantic love: The Romeo and Juliet effect. *Journal of Personality and Social Psychology*, 24, 1–10.

Duck, S. W. (1973). *Personal Relationships and Personal Constructs: A Study of Friendship Formation*. Chichester: Wiley.

(1977a). *The Study of Acquaintance*. Farnborough: Gower.

(1977b). Preface. In S. W. Duck (ed.) *Theory and Practice in Interpersonal Attraction*. London: Academic Press.

(1980a). Personal relationships in the 1980s: Toward an understanding of complex human sociality. *Western Journal of Speech Communication*, 44, 114–19.

(1980b). Taking the past to heart: One of the futures of social psychology. In R. Gilmour and S. W. Duck (eds) *The Development of Social Psychology*. London: Academic Press.

(1982a). A topography of relationship disengagement and dissolution. In S. W. Duck (ed.) *Personal Relationships 4: Dissolving Personal Relationships*. London and New York: Academic Press.

(ed.) (1982b). *Personal Relationships 4: Dissolving Personal Relationships*. London and New York: Academic Press.

(1983). *Friends for Life*. Brighton: Harvester.

(1984a). A perspective on the repair of personal relationships. In S. W. Duck (ed.) *Personal Relationships 5: Repairing Personal Relationships*. London and New York: Academic Press.

(ed.) (1984b). *Personal Relationships 5: Repairing Personal Relationships*. London and New York: Academic Press.

(1985). Social and personal relationships. In M. L. Knapp and G. R. Miller (eds) *Handbook of Interpersonal Communication*. Beverly Hills, CA: Sage.

(1986). *Human Relationships: An Introduction to Social Psychology*. London: Sage.

(1987a). How to lose friends without influencing anybody. In M. E. Roloff and G. R. Miller (eds) *Explorations in Interpersonal Communication*. Newbury Park: Sage.

(1987b). Adding apples and oranges: Investigators' implicit theories about personal relationships. In R. Burnett, P. McGhee, and D. Clarke (eds) *Accounting for relationships*. London: Methuen.

(in preparation). *Children's Friendship*. Manuscript in preparation.

Duck, S. W., Hay, D. F., Hobfoll, S. E. Ickes, W., and Montgomery, B. M. (eds) (1988). *Handbook of Personal Relationships*. Chichester: Wiley.

Duck, S. W. and Condra, M. B. (in preparation). Stimulus deficient communication: An investigation of the Goldman effect. University of Iowa.

Duck, S. W. and Cortez, C. (in preparation). The heart is a lonely hunter: Dating and the lonely.

Duck, S. W., and Craig, G. (1978). Personality similarity and the development of friendship: A longitudinal study. *British Journal of Social and Clinical Psychology*, 17, 237–42.

Duck, S. W. and Gilmour, R. (1981a). *Personal Relationships 1: Studying Personal Relationships*. London: Academic Press.

(1981b). *Personal Relationships 2: Developing Personal Relationships*. London: Academic Press.

(1981c). *Personal Relationships 3: Personal Relationships in Disorder*. London: Academic Press.

Duck, S. W. and Miell, D. E. (1984). Toward an understanding of relationship development and breakdown. In H. Tajfel, C. Fraser, and J. Jaspars (eds) *The Social Dimension: European Perspectives on Social Psychology*. Cambridge: Cambridge University Press.

(1986). Charting the development of personal relationships. In R. Gilmour and S. W. Duck (eds) *The Emerging Field of Personal Relationships*. Hillsdale, NJ: Lawrence Erlbaum.

Duck, S. W. and Perlman, D. (1985). The thousand islands of personal relationships: A prescriptive analysis for future explorations. In S. W. Duck and D. Perlman (eds) *Understanding Personal Relationships Research: An Interdisciplinary Approach*. London: Sage.

Duck, S. W. and Pond, K. (1988) Friends, Romans, countrymen, lend me your restrospections accounts: Rhetoric and reality in personal relationships. In C. Hendrick (ed.) *Review of Personality and Social Psychology*, vol. 10, *Close Relationships*. Beverly Hills, CA: Sage.

Duck, S. W. and Sants, H. K. A. (1983). On the origin of the specious: Are personal relationships really interpersonal states? *Journal of Social and Clinical Psychology*, 1, 27–41.

Duck, S. W. and Spencer, C. P. (1972). Personal constructs and friendship formation. *Journal of Personality and Social Psychology*, 23, 40–5.

Dunn, J. (1988) Relations among relationships. In S. W. Duck, D. F. Hay, S. E. Hobfoll, W. Ickes and B. M. Montgomery (eds) *Handbook of Personal Relationships*. Chichester: Wiley.

Dunn, J. and Kendrick, C. (1982). *Siblings: Love, Envy and Understanding*. London: Grant McIntyre.

Dutton, D. and Aron, A. (1974) Some evidence for heightened sexual attraction under conditions of high anxiety. *Journal of Personality and Social Psychology*, 30, 510–17.

Edwards, D. and Middleton, D. (1988). Conversational remembering and family relationships: How children learn to remember. *Journal of Social and Personal Relationships*, 5, 3–25.

Ehrlich, H. J. and Lipsey, C. (1969). Affective style as a variable in person perception. *Journal of Personality*, 37, 522–40.

Eiser, J. R. (1980). Prolegomena to a more applied social psychology. In R. Gilmour and S. W. Duck (eds) *The Development of Social Psychology*. London: Academic Press.

Emler, N. and Fisher, S. (1982). Gossip and social participation. Paper presented to Social Psychology Section of BPS, Oxford, September.

Farrell, J. and Markman, H. J. (1986). Individual and interpersonal factors in the etiology of marital distress: The example of re-marital couples. In R. Gilmour and S. W. Duck (eds) *The Emerging Field of Personal Relationships*. Hillsdale, NJ: Erlbaum.

Ferreira, A. and Winter, W. (1974). On the nature of marital relationships: Measurable differences in spontaneous agreement. *Family Process*, 13, 355–69.

Fichten, C. S. and Wright, J. (1985). Problem-solving skills in happy and distressed couples: Effects of videotape and verbal feedback. *Journal of Clinical Psychology*, 39, 157–88.

Filsinger, E. E. and Lewis, R. A. (1981). *Assessing Marriage: New Behavioral Approaches*. Beverly Hills, CA: Sage.

Fischer, C. (1982). *To Dwell among Friends*. Chicago, IL: Chicago University Press.

Fitzpatrick, M. A. and Badzinski, D. (1985). All in the family: Interpersonal communication in kin relationships. In M. L. Knapp and G. R. Miller (eds) *Handbook of Interpersonal Communication*. Beverly Hills, CA: Sage.

Foot, H. C., Chapman, A. J., and Smith, J. R. (1980). Patterns of interaction in children's friendships. In H. C. Foot, A. J. Chapman, and J. R. Smith (eds) *Friendship and Social Relations in Children*. Chichester: Wiley.

Franzoi, S. L. and Herzog, M. E. (1987). Judging physical attractiveness: What body aspects do we use? *Personality and Social Psychology Bulletin*, 13, 34–44.

Freedman, R. (1986). *Beauty Bound*. Lexington, MA: Gower.

Garfield, S. L. and Bergin, J. (eds) (1986). *Handbook of Psychotherapy and Behavior Change*. 3rd edn New York: Wiley.

Gergen, K. (1980). Toward intellectual audacity in social psychology. In R. Gilmour and S. W. Duck (eds) *The Development of Social Psychology*. London: Academic Press.

Gergen, K. and Gergen, M. (1987). Narratives of relationship. In R. Burnett, P. McGhee, and D. D. Clarke (eds) *Accounting for Relationships: Explanation, Representation and Knowledge*. London: Methuen.

Ginsburg, G. P. (1988). Rules, scripts and prototypes in personal relationships. In S. W. Duck, D. F. Hay, S. E. Hobfoll, W. Ickes and B. M. Montgomery (eds) *Handbook of Personal Relationships*. Chichester: Wiley.

Glidewell, J. C., Tucker, S., Todt, M., and Cox, S. (1982). Professional support systems: The teaching profession. In A. Nadler, J. P. Fisher, and B. M. DePaulo (eds) *Applied Research in Help-Seeking and Reactions to Aid*. New York: Academic Press.

Goffman, E. (1952). On cooling the mark out. Pelican: Harmondsworth.

Goldstein, J. W. and Rosenfeld, H. M. (1969). Insecurity and preference for persons similar to oneself. *Journal of Personality*, 37, 253–68.

Gottlieb, B. H. (1976). Lay influences on the utilization and provision of health services: A review. *Canadian Psychological Review*, 17, 126–36.

(1985). Social support and the study of personal relationships. *Journal of Social and Personal Relationships*, 2, 351–75.

(1988). Support interventions: A typology and agenda for research. In S. W. Duck, D. F. Hay, S. E. Hobfoll, W. Ickes and B. M. Montgomery (eds) *Handbook of Personal Relationships*. Chichester: Wiley.

Gottman, J. M. (1979). *Marital Interaction: Experimental Investigations*. New York: Academic Press.

Gottman, J. M., Notarius, C., Gonso, J., and Markman, H. (1976). *A Couple's Guide to Communication*. Champaign, IL: Research Press.

Gouldner, A. W. (1960). The norm of reciprocity: A preliminary statement. *American Sociological Review*, 25, 161–78.

Gurman, A. S. and Kniskern, O. P. (eds) (1981). *Handbook of Family Therapy*. New York: Brunner/Mazel.

Hagestad, G. O. and Smyer, M. (1982). Dissolving long term relationships: Patterns of divorcing in middle age. In S. W. Duck (ed.) *Personal Relationships 4: Dissolving Personal Relationships*. London and New York: Academic Press.

Haley, J. (1964). Research on family patterns: An instrument measurement. *Family Process*, 3, 41–65.

Harre, R. (1977). Friendship as an accomplishment. In S. W. Duck (ed.) *Theory and Practice in Interpersonal Attraction*. London: Academic Press.

Harrison, A. A. and Saeed, L. (1977). Let's make a deal: An analysis of revelations and stipulations in lonely hearts advertisements. *Journal of Personality and Social Psychology*, 35, 257–64.

Harvey, J. H., Hendrick, S. S., and Tucker, K. (1988). Self-report methods in studying personal relationships. In S. W. Duck, D. F. Hay, S. E. Hobfoll, W. Ickes and B. M. Montgomery (eds) *Handbook of Personal Relationships*. Chichester: Wiley.

Harvey, J. H., Weber, A. L., Galvin, K. S., Huszti, H. C., and Garnick, N. N. (1986). Attribution and the termination of close relationships: A special focus on the account. In R. Gilmour and S. W. Duck (eds) *The Emerging Field of Personal Relationships*. Hillsdale, NJ: Lawrence Erlbaum.

Harvey, J. H., Weber, A. L., Yarkin, K. L., and Stewart, B. E. (1982). An attributional approach to relationship breakdown and dissolution. In S. W. Duck (ed.) *Personal Relationships 4: Dissolving Personal Relationships*. London and New York: Academic Press.

Hatfield, E. and Traupmann, J. (1981). Intimate relationships: A perspective from equity theory. In S. W. Duck and R. Gilmour (eds) *Personal Relationships 1: Studying Personal Relationships*. London: Academic Press.

Hays, R. B. (1984). The development and maintenance of friendship. *Journal of Social and Personal Relationships*, 1, 75–98.

(1985). A longitudinal study of friendship development. *Journal of Personality and Social Psychology*, 48, 909–24.

(1988). Friendship. In S. W. Duck, D. F. Hay, S. E. Hobfoll, W. Ickes and B. M. Montgomery (eds) *Handbook of Personal Relationships*. Chichester: Wiley.

Hazan, C. and Shaver, P. (1987). Romantic love conceptualized as an attachment process. *Journal of Personality and Social Psychology*, 52(3), 511–24.

Helgeson, V. S., Shaver, P., and Dyer, M. (1987). Prototypes of intimacy and distance in same-sex and opposite-sex relationships. *Journal of Social and Personal Relationships*, 4, 195–234.

Hendrick, C. (1988). Roles and gender in relationships. In S. W. Duck, D. F. Hay, S. E. Hobfoll, W. Ickes and B. M. Montgomery (eds) *Handbook of Personal Relationships*. Chichester: Wiley.

Hendrick, C. and Brown, S. R. (1971). Introversion, extraversion and interpersonal attraction. *Journal of Personality and Social Psychology*, 20, 31–6.

Hendrick, C. and Hendrick, S. S. (1983). *Liking, Loving, and Relating*. Monterey, CA: Brooks/Cole.

(1988) Lovers wear rose coloured glasses. *Journal of Social and Personal Relationships*, 5, 161–83.

Hendrick, C., Hendrick, S. S., Foote, F. H., and Slapion-Foote, M. J. (1984). Do men and women love differently? *Journal of Social and Personal Relationships*, 1, 177–95.

Hepburn, J. R. and Crepin, A. E. (1984) Relationship strategies in a coercive institution: A study of dependence among prisoners and guards. *Journal of Social and Personal Relationships*, 1, 139–58.

Hill, C. T., Rubin, Z., and Peplau, L. A. (1976). Breakups before marriage: The end of 103 affairs. *Journal of Social Issues*, 32, 147–68.

Hinde, R. A. (1979). *Towards Understanding Relationships*. London: Academic Press.

—— (1981). The bases of a science of interpersonal relationships. In S. W. Duck and R. Gilmour (eds) *Personal Relationships 1: Studying Personal Relationships*. London: Academic Press.

Hobfoll, S. E. and Stokes, J. (1988). The processes and mechanics of social support. In S. W. Duck, D. F. Hay, S. E. Hobfoll, W. Ickes and B. M. Montgomery (eds) *Handbook of Personal Relationships*. Chichester: Wiley.

Homans, G. C. (1961). *Social Behavior: Its Elementary Forms*. London: Routledge & Kegan Paul.

Hopper, R. and Bell, R. A. (1984). Broadening the deception construct. *Quarterly Journal of Speech*, 70, 288–302.

Hopper, R., Knapp, M. L., and Scott, L. (1981). Couples' personal idioms: Exploring intimate talk. *Journal Communication*, 31, 23–33.

Horton, D. and Wohl, R. R. (1956). Mass communication and parasocial interaction: Observations on intimacy at a distance. *Psychiatry*, 19, 215–29.

Huesmann, L. R. and Levinger, G. (1976). Incremental exchange theory: A formal model for progression in dyadic social interaction. In L. Berkowitz and E. Walster (eds) *Advances in Experimental Social Psychology*. New York: Academic Press.

Huston, T. L. and Levinger, G. (1978). Interpersonal attraction and relationships. In M. R. Rosenzweig and L. W. Porter (eds) *Annual Review of Psychology*, vol. 29. Palo Alto, CA: Annual Reviews.

Huston, T. L., Surra, C. A., Fitzgerald, N. M., and Cate, R. M. (1981). From courtship to marriage: Mate selection as an interpersonal process. In S. W. Duck and R. Gilmour (eds) *Personal Relationships 2: Developing Personal Relationships*. London: Academic Press.

Ickes, W. and Tooke, W. (1988). The observational method: Studying the interaction of minds and bodies. In S. W. Duck, D. F. Hay, S. E. Hobfoll, W. Ickes and B. M. Montgomery (eds) *Handbook of Personal Relationships*. Chichester: Wiley.

Jaffe, D. T. and Kanter, R. M. (1979). Couple strains in communal households: A four-factor model of the separation process. In G. Levinger and O. Moles (eds) *Divorce and Separation*. New York: Basic Books.

Johnson, M. P. (1982). Social and cognitive features of the dissolution of commitment to relationships. In S. W. Duck (ed.) *Personal Relationships 4: Dissolving Personal Relationships.* London: Academic Press.

Jones, E. E. and Gordon, E. M. (1972). Timing of self disclosure and its effect on self disclosure. *Journal of Personality and Social Psychology,* 24, 358–65.

Jones, W. H. and Perlman, D. (eds) (1987). *Advances in Personal Relationships.* Greenwich: JAI Press.

Jones, W. H., Cavert, C. W., Snider, R. C., and Bruce, T. (1985). Relational stress: An analysis of situations and events associated with loneliness. In S. W. Duck and D. Perlman (eds) *Understanding Personal Relationships Research: An Interdisciplinary Approach.* London: Sage.

Jones, W. H., Hansson, R. O., and Cutrona, C. (1984). Helping the lonely: Issues of intervention with young and older adults. In S. W. Duck (ed.) *Personal Relationships 5: Repairing Personal Relationships.* London and New York: Academic Press.

Jourard, S. M. (1964). *The Transparent Self.* New York: Van Nostrand.

Kaplan, R. E. (1976). Maintaining interpersonal relationships: A bipolar theory. *Interpersonal Development,* 6, 106–19.

  (1984). Repairing ailing work relationships. In S. W. Duck (ed.) *Personal Relationships 5: Repairing Personal Relationships.* London and New York: Academic Press.

Kelley, H. H., Berscheid, E., Christensen, A., Harvey, J. H., Huston, T. L., Levinger, G., McClintock, E., Peplau, L. A., and Peterson, D. R. (1983). *Close Relationships.* San Francisco, CA: Freeman.

Kelly, C., Huston, T. L., and Cate, R. M. (1985). Premarital relationship correlates of the erosion of satisfaction in marriage. *Journal of Social and Personal Relationships,* 2, 167–78.

Kelvin, P. (1977). Predictability, power and vulnerability in interpersonal attraction. In S. W. Duck (ed.) *Theory and Practice in Interpersonal Attraction.* London: Academic Press.

Kenny, D. A. (1988). The analysis of data from two person relationships. In S. W. Duck, D. F. Hay, S. E. Hobfoll, W. Ickes and B. M. Montgomery (eds) *Handbook of Personal Relationships.* Chichester: Wiley.

Kephart, W. M. (1967). Some correlates of romantic love. *Journal of Marriage and the Family,* 29, 470–4.

Kerckhoff, A. C. (1974). The social context of interpersonal attraction. In T. L. Huston (ed.) *Foundations of Interpersonal Attraction.* New York: Academic Press.

Kerckhoff, A. C. and Davis, K. E. (1962). Value consensus and need complementarity in mate selection. *American Sociological Review,* 27, 295–303.

Kidd, V. (1975). Happily ever after and other relationships styles: Advice on interpersonal relations in popular magazines, 1951–1972. *Quarterly Journal of Speech,* 61, 31–9.

Klinger, E. (1977). *Meaning and Void: Inner Experience and the Incentives in People's Lives*. Minneapolis, MN: University of Minnesota Press.

Knapp, M. L. (1984). *Interpersonal Communication and Human Relationships*. Boston, MA: Allyn & Bacon.

Koestner, R. and Wheeler, L. (1988) Self presentation in personal advertisements: The influence of implicit norms of attraction and role expectations. *Journal of Social and Personal Relationships*, 5, 149–60.

Krebs, D. and Adinolfi, A. A. (1975) Physical attractiveness, social relations, and personality style. *Journal of Personality and Social Psychology*, 31, 245–53.

Kurth, S. B. (1970). Friendship and friendly relations. In G. J. McCall, M. M. McCall, N. K. Denzin, G. D. Suttles, and S. B. Kurth, *Social Relationships*. Chicago, IL: Aldine.

LaGaipa, J. J. (1977). Testing a multidimensional approach to friendship. In S. W. Duck (ed.) *Theory and Practice in Interpersonal Attraction*. London: Academic Press.

     (1982). Rules and rituals in disengaging from relationships. In S. W. Duck (ed.) *Personal Relationships 4: Dissolving Personal Relationships*. London and New York: Academic Press.

Laner, M. R. (1985) Unpleasant aggressive and abusive activities in courtship: A comparison of Mormon and non-Mormon college students. *Deviant Behavior*, 6, 145–68.

Lea, M. and Duck, S. W. (1982). A model for the role of similarity of values in friendship development. *British Journal of Social Psychology*, 21, 301–10.

Leary, M. R. (1983). *Understanding Social Anxiety: Social, Personality and Clinical Perspectives*. Beverly Hills, CA: Sage.

Leary, M. R., Rogers, P. A., Canfield, R. W., and Coe, C. (1986). Boredom in interpersonal encounters: Antecedents and social implications. *Journal of Personality and Social Psychology*, 51, 968–75.

Lee, J. A. (1973). *The Colors of Love: An Exploration of Ways of Loving*. Don Mills, Ontario: New Press.

Lee, L. (1984). Sequences in separation: A framework for investigating endings of the personal (romantic) relationship. *Journal of Social and Personal Relationships*, 1, 49–74.

Levinger, G. (1979). A social exchange view of the dissolution of pair relationships. In R. L. Burgess and T. L. Huston (eds) *Social Exchange: Advances in Theory and Research*. New York: Academic Press.

Levinger, G. and Breedlove, J. (1966). Interpersonal attraction and agreement: A study of marriage partners. *Journal of Personality and Social Psychology*, 3, 367–72.

Levinger, G., Senn, D., and Jorgensen, B. W. (1970) Progress towards permanence in courtship: A test of the Kerckhoff–Davis hypothesis. *Sociometry*, 33, 427–43.

Lewis, C. N. and O'Brien, M. (1987). *Reassessing Fatherhood: New Observations on Fathers and the Modern Family*. London: Sage.

Lewis, R. A. (1973). Societal reaction and the formation of dyads. *Soci-ometry*, **36**, 409–18.

(1978). Emotional intimacy among men. *Journal of Social Issues*, **34**, 108–21.

Lewis, R. A. and McAvoy, P. (1984). Improving the quality of relationships: Therapeutic intervention with opiate abusing couples. In S. W. Duck (ed.) *Personal Relationships 5: Repairing Personal Relationships*. London and New York: Academic Press.

Lips, H. M. and Morrison, A. (1986) Changes in the sense of family among couples having their first child. *Journal of Social and Personal Relationships*, **3**, 393–400.

Little, B. R. (1984). Personal project analysis. Paper presented to Conference on the Self, Cardiff.

Livingstone, S. (1987). The representation of personal relationships in TV drama: Realism, convention and morality. In R. Burnett, P. McGhee, and D. D. Clarke (eds) *Accounting for Relationships: Explanation, Representation and Knowledge*. London: Methuen.

Lloyd, S. A. and Cate, R. M. (1985). The developmental course of conflict in premarital relationship dissolution. *Journal of Social and Personal Relationships*, **2**, 179–94.

Lund, M. (1985). The development of investment and commitment scales for predicting continuity of personal relationships. *Journal of Social and Personal Relationships*, **2**, 3–23.

Lynch, J. (1977). *The Broken Heart: Medical Consequences of Loneliness*. New York: Basic Books.

Lynn, S. and Bolig, R. (1985). Personal advertisements: Sources of data about relationships. *Journal of Social and Personal Relationships*, **2**, 377–83.

McAdams, D. (1988) Personal needs and personal relationships. In S. W. Duck, D. F. Hay, S. E. Hobfoll, W. Ickes and B. M. Montgomery (eds) *Handbook of Personal Relationships*. Chichester: Wiley.

McCall, G. J. (1970). The social organization of relationships. In G. J. McCall, M. M. McCall, N. K. Denzin, G. D. Suttles, and S. B. Kurth, *Social Relationships*. Chicago, IL: Aldine.

(1982). Becoming unrelated: The management of bond dissolution. In S. W. Duck (ed.) *Personal Relationships 4: Dissolving Personal Relationships*. London and New York: Academic Press.

(1988). The organisational life cycle of relationships. In S. W. Duck, D. F. Hay, S. E. Hobfoll, W. Ickes, and B. M. Montgomery (eds) *Handbook of Personal Relationships*. Chichester: Wiley.

Mace, D. and Mace, V. (1974). *We Can Have Better Marriages If We Really Want Them*. Abingdon: Nashville.

Makepeace, J. M. (1981) Courtship violence among college students. *Family Relations*, **30**, 97–102.

Margolin, G. (1983). An interactional model for the behavioral assessment of marital relationships. *Behavioural Assessments*, 5 (2), 103–27.

Marshall, L. and Rose, P. (1987). Gender stress and violence in the adult relationships of a sample of college students. *Journal of Social and Personal Relationships*, 4, 299–316.

Marston, P. J., Hecht, M. L., and Robers, T. (1987) "True love ways": The subjective experience and communication of romantic love. *Journal of Social and Personal Relationships*, 4, 387–408.

Masters, W. H. and Johnson, V. (1970). *Human Sexual Inadequacy*. Boston, MA: Little, Brown.

Mehrabian, A. (1972). *Nonverbal Communication*. Chicago, IL: Aldine Atherton.

Mehrabian, A. and Ksionzky, S. (1974). *A Theory of Affiliation*. Lexington, MA: Lexington Books.

Michaels, J. W., Acock, A. C., and Edwards, J. N. (1986). Social exchange and equity determinants of relationship commitment. *Journal of Social and Personal Relationships*, 3, 161–76.

Miell, D. E. (1984). Strategies of self disclosure. Unpublished Ph.D. dissertation, University of Lancaster, UK.

(1987). Memory for relationship development: Constructing a context for interaction. In R. Burnett, P. McGhee, and D. D. Clarke (eds) *Accounting for Relationships: Explanation, Representation and Knowledge*. London: Methuen.

Miell, D. E. and Duck, S. W. (1986) Strategies in developing friendship. In V. J. Derlega and B. A. Winstead (eds) *Friendship and Social Interaction*. New York: Springer-Verlag.

Milardo, R. M. (1982). Friendship networks in developing relationships: Converging and diverging social environments. *Social Psychology Quarterly*, 45, 162–72.

Milardo, R. M., Johnson, M. P., and Huston, T. L. (1983). Developing close relationships: Changing patterns of interaction between pair members and social networks. *Journal of Personality and Social Psychology*, 44, 964–76.

Miller, G. R. and Parks, M. R. (1982). Communication in dissolving relationships. In S. W. Duck (ed.) *Personal Relationships 4: Dissolving Personal Relationships*. London and New York: Academic Press.

Miller, G. R., Mongeau, P. A., and Sleight, C. (1986). Fudging with friends and lying to lovers: Deceptive communication in interpersonal relationships. *Journal of Social and Personal Relationships*, 3, 495–512.

Montgomery, B. M. (1981). Verbal immediacy as a behavioral indicator of open communication content. *Communication Quarterly*, 30, 28–34.

(1986). Interpersonal attraction as a function of open communication and gender. *Communication Research Reports*, 3, 343–62.

(1988). Quality communication in personal relationships. In S. W. Duck, D. F. Hay, S. E. Hobfoll, W. Ickes and B. M. Montgomery (eds) *Handbook of Personal Relationships*. Chichester: Wiley.

Moore, J. S., Graziano, W., and Millar, M. G. (1987). Physical attractiveness, sex role orientation and the evaluation of adults and children. *Personality and Social Psychology Bulletin*, 13, 95–102.

Morgan, D. L. (1986). Personal relationships as an interface between social networks and social cognitions. *Journal of Social and Personal Relationships*, 3, 403–22.

Morton, T. L. and Douglas, M. A. (1981). Growth of relationships. In S. W. Duck and R. Gilmour (eds) *Personal Relationships 2: Developing Personal Relationships*. London: Academic Press.

Morton, T. L., Alexander, J. F., and Altman, I. (1976). Communication and relationship definition. In G. R. Miller (ed.) *Exploration in Interpersonal Communication*. Beverly Hills, CA: Sage.

Mott, F. L. and Moore, S. F. (1979). The causes of marital disruption among young American women: An interdisciplinary perspective. *Journal of Marriage and the Family*, 41, 335–65.

Murstein, B. I. (1971). A theory of marital choice and its applicability to marriage adjustment. In B. I. Murstein (ed.) *Theories of attraction and Love*, New York: Springer.

(1976). *Who Will Marry Whom?* New York: Springer.

(1977). The Stimulus-Value-Role (SVR) theory of dyadic relationships. In S. W. Duck (ed.) *Theory and Practice in Interpersonal Attraction*. London: Academic Press.

Murstein, B. I. and Glaudin, V. (1968). The use of the MMPI in the determination of marital maladjustment. *Journal of Marriage and the Family*, 30, 651–5.

Neimeyer, G. J. and Hudson, J. E. (1985). Couple's constructs: Personal systems in marital satisfaction. In D. Bannister (ed.) *Issues and Approaches in Personal Construct Theory*. London: Academic Press.

Newcomb, M. D. (1986). Cohabitation, marriage and divorce among adolescents and young adults. *Journal of Social and Personal Relationships*, 3, 473–94.

Newcomb, M. D. and Bentler, P. M. (1981). Marital breakdown. In S. W. Duck and R. Gilmour (eds) *Personal Relationships 3: Personal Relationships in Disorder*. London: Academic Press.

Newcomb, T. (1961). *The Acquaintance Process*. New York: Holt, Rinehart.

Noller, P. (1985). Negative communications in marriage. *Journal of Social and Personal Relationships*, 2, 289–301.

Noller, P. and Venardos, C. (1986). Communication awareness in married couples. *Journal of Social and Personal Relationships*, 3, 31–42.

Norton, A. J. and Moorman, J. E. (1987). Current trends in marriage and divorce among American Women. *Journal of Marriage and the Family*, 49, 3–14.

Norton, R. (1983). *Communicator Style: Theory, Applications, and Measures*. Beverly Hills, CA: Sage.

O'Connell, L. (1984) An exploration of exchange in three social relationships: Kinship, friendship and the market place. *Journal of Social and Personal Relationships*, 1, 333–45.

O'Connor, P. and Brown, G. W. (1984). Supportive relationships: Fact or fancy? *Journal of Social and Personal Relationships*, 1, 159–76.

Olson, D. H. (1977). Insiders' and outsiders' views of relationships: Research studies. In G. Levinger and H. L. Raush (eds) *Close Relationships: Perspectives on the Meaning of Intimacy*. Amherst, MA: University of Massachusetts Press.

Orford, J. and O'Reilly, P. (1981). Disorders in the family. In S. W. Duck and R. Gilmour (eds) *Personal Relationships 3: Personal Relationships in Disorder*. London: Academic Press.

Parks, M. R. and Adelman. M. (1983). Communication networks and the development of romantic relationships: An expansion of uncertainty reduction theory. *Human Communication Research*, 10, 55–79.

Patterson, G. R. (1988). Functions of nonverbal behavior in close relationships. In S. W. Duck, D. F. Hay, S. E. Hobfoll, W. Ickes and B. M. Montgomery (eds) *Handbook of Personal Relationships*. Chichester: Wiley.

Peplau, L. A. and Perlman, D. (1982). Perspectives on loneliness. In L. A. Peplau and D. Perlman (eds) *Loneliness: A Sourcebook of Current Theory, Research and Therapy*. New York: Wiley.

Perlman, D. (1986). Chance and coincidence in relationships. Paper presented at the International Conference on Personal Relationships, Tel Aviv, Israel.

Perlman, D. and Duck, S. W. (eds) (1987). *Intimate Relationships: Development, Dynamics, and Deterioration*. Beverly Hills, CA: Sage.

Perlman, D. and Fehr, B. (1987). The development of intimate relationships. In D. Perlman and S. W. Duck (eds) *Intimate Relationships: Development, Dynamics and Deterioration*. Beverly Hills, CA: Sage.

Perrin, F. A. C. (1921). Physical attractiveness and repulsions. *Journal of Experimental Psychology*, 4, 203–17.

Pilisuk, M. and Minkler, M. (1980). Supportive networks: Life ties for the elderly. *Journal of Social Issues*, 36, 95–116.

Planalp, S. and Honeycutt, J. M. (1985). Events that increase uncertainty in personal relationships. *Human Communication Research*, 11, 593–604.

Platt, J. J. and Labate, C. (1976). *Heroin Addiction: The Research and Treatment*. New York: Wiley.

Reis, H. T. (1984). Social interaction and well-being. In S. W. Duck (ed.) *Personal Relationships 5: Repairing Personal Relationships*. London and New York: Academic Press.

Reis, H. T. and Shaver, P. (1988). Intimacy as an interpersonal process. In S. W. Duck, D. F. Hay, S. E. Hobfoll, W. Ickes and B. M. Montgomery (eds) *Handbook of Personal Relationships*. Chichester: Wiley.

Reis, H. T., Nezlek, J., and Wheeler, L. (1980). Physical attractiveness and social interaction. *Journal of Personality and Social Psychology*, 38, 604–17.

Reisman, J. M. (1981). Adult friendships. In S. W. Duck and R. Gilmour (eds) *Personal Relationships 2: Developing Personal Relationships*. London: Academic Press.

Renne, K. S. (1970). Correlates of dissatisfaction in marriage. *Journal of Marriage and the Family*, 32, 54–67.

Richardson, H. M. (1939). Studies of mental resemblance between husbands and wives and between friends. *Psychological Bulletin*, 36, 104–20.

Ridley, C. A. and Nelson, R. R. (1984). The behavioral effects of training premarital couples in mutual problem solving skills. *Journal of Social and Personal Relationships*, 1, 197–210.

Riggio, R. E. and Woll, S. (1984). The role of nonverbal cues and physical attractiveness in the selection of dating partners. *Journal of Social and Personal Relationships*, 1, 347–57.

Rodin, M. J. (1982). Non-engagement, failure to engage, and disengagement. In S. W. Duck (ed.) *Personal Relationships 4: Dissolving Personal Relationships*. London and New York: Academic Press.

Rogers, W. and Thornton, A. (1985) Changing patterns of first marriage in the United States. *Demography*, 22, 265–79.

Rose, S. and Serafica, F. C. (1986). Keeping and ending casual, close and best friendships. *Journal of Social and Personal Relationships*, 3, 275–88.

Ross, M. D. and McFarland, C. (1988). Constructing the past: Biasses in personal memory. In D. Bar-Tal and A. Kruglanski (eds) *Social Psychology of Knowledge*, Cambridge: Cambridge University Press.

Rubin, A. M., Perse, E. M., and Powell, R. A. (1985). Loneliness, parasocial interaction and local TV news viewing. *Human Communication Research*, 12, 155–80.

Rubin, Z. (1970) Measurement of romantic love. *Journal of Personality and Social Psychology*, 16, 265–73.

Rubin, Z. and Levinger, G. (1974). Theory and data badly mated: A critique of Murstein's SVR and Lewis's PDF models of mate selection. *Journal of Marriage and the Family*, 36, 226–31.

Rusbult, C. E. (1987) Responses to dissatisfaction in close relationships: The Exit-Voice-Loyalty-Neglect model. In D. Perlman and S. W. Duck (eds) *Intimate Relationships: Development, Dynamics, and Deterioration*. Beverly Hills, CA: Sage.

Rychlak, J. (1984). Relationship theory: An historical development in psychology leading to a teleological image of humanity. *Journal of Social and Personal Relationships*, 1, 363–86.

Sabatelli, R. and Pearce, J. (1986). Exploring marital expectations. *Journal of Social and Personal Relationships*, 3, 307–22.

Sabini, J. and Silver, M. (1982). *Moralities of everyday life*. Oxford: Oxford University Press.

Sants, H. K. A. (1984). Conceptions of friendship, social behaviour and school achievements in six-year-old children. *Journal of Social and Personal Relationships*, 1, 293–309.

Schachter, S. (1959). *The Psychology of Affiliation*. Stanford, CA: Stanford University Press.

Shakespeare, W. (1599). Hamlet, the Prince of Denmark: A field study and factorial analysis of relational exchange and ontological questions. *Journal of Personality and Social Psychology*, 570, 1–329.

Shaver, P., Furman, W., and Buhrmester, D. (1985). Aspects of a life transition: Network changes, social skills and loneliness. In S. W. Duck and D. Perlman (eds) *Understanding Personal Relationships Research: An Interdisciplinary Approach*. London: Sage.

Shea, B. C. and Pearson, J. C. (1986). The effects of relationship type, partner intent, and gender on the selection of relationship maintenance strategies. *Communication Monographs*, 53, 352–64.

Simmel, G. (1908/1950). *The Sociology of Georg Simmel* (trans. Kurt Wolff). New York: Free Press.

Simpson, J. A., Campbell, B., and Berscheid, E. (1986). The association between romantic love and marriage: Kephart (1967) twice revisited. *Personality and Social Psychology Bulletin*, 12, 363–72.

Snyder, M. and Smith, D. (1986) Personality and friendship: The friendship worlds of self monitors. In V. J. Derlega and B. A. Winstead (eds) *Friendship and Social Interaction*. New York: Springer-Verlag.

Sprecher, S. (1987). The effects of self disclosure given and received on affection for an intimate partner and stability of the relationship. *Journal of Social and Personal Relationships*, 4, 115–28.

Sterk, H. (1986). Functioning fictions: The adjustment rhetoric of Silhouette romance novels. Unpublished Ph.D. thesis, University of Iowa.

Sternberg, R. J. (1987) Explorations of love. In W. H. Jones and D. Perlman (eds) *Advances in Personal Relationships*, vol. 1. Greenwich: JAI Press.

Sternberg, R. J. and Grajek, S. (1984) The nature of love. *Journal of Personality and Social Psychology*, 47, 312–29.

Stroebe, W. (1977) Self esteem and interpersonal attraction. In S. W. Duck (ed.) *Theory and Practice in Interpersonal Attraction*. London: Academic Press.

Stueve, C. A. and Gerson, K. (1977). Personal relations across the life cycle. In C. S. Fischer (ed.) *Networks and Places: Social Relations in the Urban Setting*. New York: Free Press.

Suls, J. M. (1977). Gossip as social comparison. *Journal of Communication*, 27, 164–72.

Surra, C. A. (1987). Reasons for changes in commitment: Variations by courtship type. *Journal of Social and Personal Relationships*, 4, 17–34.

Surra, C. A., Arizzi, P., and Asmussen, L. A. (1988). The association between reasons for commitment and the development and outcome of marital relationships. *Journal of Social and Personal Relationships.* 5, 47–64.

Swensen, C. H. (1972). The behavior of love. In H. A. Otto (ed.) *Love Today.* New York: Associated Press.

Tesser, A. and Paulhus, D. (1976). Toward a causal model of love. *Journal of Personality and Social Psychology,* 34, 1095–105.

Thibaut, J. W. and Kelley, H. H. (1959). *The Social Psychology of Groups.* New York: Wiley.

Van Lear, A. and Trujillo, N. (1986). On becoming acquainted: A longitudinal study of social judgement processes. *Journal of Social and Personal Relationships,* 3, 375–92.

Vaughn, D. (1986). *Uncoupling: Turning Points in Intimate Relationships.* New York: Oxford University Press.

Walster, E. H., Walster, G. W., and Berscheid, E. (1978). *Equity Theory and Research.* Boston, MA: Allyn & Bacon.

Walster, E., Aronson, E., Abrahams, D., and Rottman, L. (1966). Importance of physical attractiveness in dating behavior. *Journal of Personality and Social Psychology,* 5, 508–16.

Weber, A. (1983). Breaking up. Paper presented to Nags Head Conference, May.

Weber, A. L., Harvey, J. H., and Stanley, M. A. (1987). The nature and motivations of accounts in failed relationships. In R. Burnett, P. McGhee, and D. D. Clarke (eds) *Accounting for Relationships: Explanations, Representation and Knowledge.* London: Methuen.

Weiss, R. A. (1974). The provisions of social relationships. In Z. Rubin (ed.) *Doing unto Others.* Englewood Cliffs, NJ: Prentice-Hall.

(1975). *Marital Separation.* New York: Basic Books.

Wellman, B. (1985). Domestic work, paid work and network. In S. W. Duck and D. Perlman (eds) *Understanding Personal Relationships Research: An Interdisciplinary Approach.* London: Sage.

White, J. M. (1985). Perceived similarity and understanding in married couples. *Journal of Social and Personal Relationships,* 2, 40–57.

Woll, S. B. (1986). So many to choose from: Decision strategies in videodating. *Journal of Social and Personal Relationships,* 3, 43–52.

Woll, S. B. and Cozby, P. C. (1987) Videodating and other alternatives to traditional methods of relationship initiation. In W. H. Jones and D. Perlman (eds) *Advances in Personal Relationships,* vol. 1. Greenwich: JAI Press.

Wright, J. and Fichten, C. S. (1976). Denial of responsibility, videotape feedback and attribution theory: Relevance for behavioral marital therapy. *Canadian Psychological Review,* 7, 219–30.

Wright, P. H. (1984). Self referent motivation and the intrinsic quality of friendship. *Journal of Social and Personal Relationships,* 1, 115–30.

(1985). The Acquaintance Description Form. In S. W. Duck and D.

Perlman (eds) *Understanding Personal Relationships Research: An Interdisciplinary Approach.* London: Sage.

Wright, R. and Contrada, R. J. (1986). Dating selectivity and interpersonal attraction: Toward a better understanding of the "Elusive Phenomenon." *Journal of Social and Personal Relationships*, 3, 131–48.

Yaffe, M. (1981). Disordered sexual relationships. In S. W. Duck and R. Gilmour (eds) *Personal Relationships 3: Personal Relationships in Disorder.* London: Academic Press.

Yogev, S. (1987). Marital satisfaction and sex role perceptions among dual-earner couples. *Journal of Social and Personal Relationships*, 4, 35–46.

Young, J. E. (1982). Loneliness, depression and cognitive therapy: Theory and application. In L. A. Peplau and D. Perlman (eds) *Loneliness: A Sourcebook of Theory, Research and Therapy.* New York: Wiley.

Zimmer, T. (1986). Premarital anxieties. *Journal of Social and Personal Relationships*, 3, 149–60.

AUTHOR INDEX

// SUBJECT INDEX